To Grandad
I hope this can [help?] ... much Grandad, you really are the best and we are lucky to have you as our Grandad + Great Grandad.
Love lots
[Carla?] + Olivia

Tinnitus, From Tyrant to Friend

How to Let Go of the Ringing in Your Ears

Julian Cowan Hill

Tinnitus, From Tyrant to Friend: How to Let Go of the Ringing in your Ears.
Second Edition

© 2010 Copyright Julian Cowan Hill

All Rights Reserved

No part of this book maybe reproduced or utilized in any form or by any means, electronic or mechanical, without premission in writing from the Publisher.

The moral right of the author has been asserted.

First published by Kindle 2015

Other books published by Julian Cowan Hill

A Positive Tinnitus Story: How I Let Go of Tinnitus the Natural Way
Published by Kindle 2014

Acknowledgements

I wish to thank all the tinnitus people I have worked with for providing a constant challenge and a source of inspiration. You have taught me what helps let go of tinnitus, and also what is not helpful. Now I can share this experience with others.

I would also like to thank the Craniosacral Therapy and Core Process Psychotherapy community of Great Britain for teaching me how to be well and let go at a deep level. It is your support, education and deep sensitivity that has opened up a whole new world of well-being for me where tinnitus cannot survive.

I am also indebted to Dharma and Dzogchen teachings for putting me in touch with what matters. May this work help free people from suffering and find the path that leads to letting go of tinnitus.

Contents

Introduction   6
   Well-Being Matrix© For Tinintus   8

Chapter 1
   Establishing the Ground   10
   Core Issue 1: Negative People   11
   What is tinnitus?   12
   Core Issue 2: Tinnitus is not an ear based problem   14

Chapter 2
   What are tinnitus people like?   17
   Core Issue 3: Silence   21
   Core Issue 4: Stop trying to cure your tinnitus   22
   Core Issue 5: Are you ready to change   25

Chapter 3
   How to make progress   27
   Core Issue 6: Moaning and groaning   28
   Core Issue 7: Avoiding doom and gloom   30
   Core Issue 8: Don't let vampires sap your energy   31
   Core Issue 9: Letting go into support   32
   Core Issue 10: Diet   34
   Core Issue 11: Exercise   35
   Core Issue 12: Getting in touch with your body   36

Chapter 4
   Charting your progress   38

Level 1 – Stuck 39
   Technique 1 – Crisis Calmer 45

Level 2 – Struggling 46
   Technique 2 – Clenching and relaxing 52

Level 3 – Resigned 56
   Technique 3 – Better and worst list 60

Level 4 – Motivated 61
   Technique 4 – Knowing what matters to you 66
   Technique 5 – How do you view yourself? 67
   Technique 6 – Running commentary 68

Level 5 – Letting Go 71
   Technique 7 – Audiovisualisation 74

Level 6 – Empowered 80
   Technique 8 – Breathing technique 85

Level 7 – Liberated 87
   Technique 9 – Orienting to midline 91

Bibliography 95

Introduction

It is my heartfelt wish that you learn how to let go of your tinnitus and feel much happier as a result. Although I cannot guarantee how long it will take or how much you will improve, if you follow these guidelines I have no doubt you will notice a difference. Please note that this book applies equally to people with Meniere's Disease.

In the first four chapters I explain the basics: what tinnitus is, why we get it and how to let go of this condition. Out of thousands of hours work I have condensed down what I consider to be 12 of the most important "Core Issues" that will help you on your journey to recovery. They are numbered in the index for easy reference.

Once these foundations are in place we move into the main part of the book where I chart the landmarks of progress you make as your tinnitus gets better. Level 1 is for people with the worst kind of tinnitus, and is called "Stuck." Level 7, at the top of the matrix is for those who have let go of tinnitus completely, and is called "Liberated." Reading through these levels, please get a sense of where you would place yourself. This will help you get a sense of what you need to focus on in order to get better.

When we first get tinnitus it often treats us like a tyrant. At Level 1 I show you how to stop it taking over your thought processes and find some space. As you make progress, you learn to accept symptoms more easily and start to realise that tinnitus is actually an incredibly useful healthometre that shows what works for you and what does not, behaving a bit like a doctor. Many people, once they get up to Level 4, feel they have made enough progress and their tinnitus is good enough not to bother working on any more. That's great. However, some people realise how useful tinnitus can be and learn to listen to their bodily reactions deeply, and go on to develop a deep sense of well-being and awareness that can benefit them for years to come, making a full recovery.

No matter how far you want to go on this journey, you will find a lot of practical advice in this book. Therefore, I suggest you read it through once, and then start again, working your way through the practice techniques thoroughly. Hopefully, by time you get to the end of this book you will have a clear sense of what really helps tinnitus, and up to what level you would like to work.

Disclaimer: please note that just reading this book alone is not likely to stop your tinnitus. You will probably feel less threatened by symptoms once you understand where they come from and why they are there. However, if you want to make good progress I encourage you to follow the advice, practise the techniques regularly, and most importantly of all, get therapeutic support. If you do this, there is every chance your tinnitus will get much better.

I have created a **Well-being Matrix for Tinnitus** © which is a chart that maps out the progress people make as they get better. The entire book is based on this Matrix set out on the next page. This will help you recognise where you are on the path of progress and where you will need to focus your energy. My aim with this chart is to show you that many people do get better and that it is a well-trodden path that you too can follow.

I am available to offer support at my clinic in London or via Skype. I can check through some of the techniques in detail with you to make sure you know what to do, and can also find a suitable practitioner near you, so that you can set out on a course of therapy that will help let go of your tinnitus.

In the meantime, I wish you well on what is in fact a voyage of self-discovery. These days I am extremely grateful for my own tinnitus for showing me how to be really well and happy in myself. I would like to share this process with you. My aim is for you to learn how to turn tinnitus into your very own healthometre and guide, leading you to a much deeper sense of well-being.

I have learnt that becoming grounded and establishing a clear sense of well-being in the body is one of the best ways to make it hard for tinnitus to keep going at the same intensity. I have also learnt that peace is an experience that we feel through our embodied awareness. In this light, I wish you peace.

Julian Cowan Hill, MA UKCP RCST

Well-being Matrix for Tinnitus ©

Level	Tinnitus is like a:	Effect on life	Feelings
7 Liberated	**Spiritual Guide** Led you to your deeper needs and appreciation of life itself	Connected you to the larger picture. Made you aware that you are creator of the way you feel.	Gratitude Humility Peace Balance Strength
6 Empowered	**Friend** Tinnitus helps you look after yourself and is a reliable positive influence	T is positive, useful and reliable part of self. Most of time not aware of it.	Empowered T is very easy to manage and never threatening
5 Letting go	**Therapist** Reflects the way you feel inside and how you treat/manage yourself	T deepens self-knowledge and ability to witness the way you are	Letting go Deep acceptance Witnessing feelings more manageably
4 Motivated	**Teacher** Shows you what helps you feel better and what makes you worse: Healthometre	Decision time – what really matters to you? What do you need to let go of?	More loving towards self. More allowing and open. Motivated independent
3 Resigned	**Doctor** Starts to accept T begrudgingly and listen to the advice it is trying to give you	Accepts that changes are needed for T to back off. Accepts support/help	Resignation Acceptance Sadness Begrudging
2 Struggling	**Sergeant Major** Bossed about by T. Frustrated with emotional struggle and relentness	Dominated by T. Copes rarely. Loathe to admit moments of being OK.	Resentment Frustration/Anger Why should I change? Why me?
1 Stuck	**Tyrant** Hopeless with no way out. Totally at the mercy of tinnitus	Most of life severely taken over. Can't get away from T. Little pleasure.	Great fear and sense of loss. No control. Powerless/hopeless

Tinnitus, From Tyrant to Friend

Mindset	Awareness	Challenge	Level
Not aware of T anymore Focused mind. Symptoms lead you back to health	Body, energy and mind are unified and integrated, and are part of larger universal field	To let go of the need to be free of tinnitus	**7** Liberated
Don't care about tinnitus anymore Can't be bothered to check on it	Really in touch with how your mind, body, energy and feelings affect each other	To let go of the need to still check if tinnitus is there	**6** Empowered
Tinnitus is no longer central issue or a problem Start forgetting about it	Realise impact of thoughts, behaviour and emotions on body and energy	To stay friends with T even when stress makes it worse	**5** Letting go
T is there but doesn't bug me so much Highlights where you need to work	Starts to take better care of self. Learns body is where issues can be processed. Mind links to body	Develop confidence in knowing it will get better and learn from mistakes	**4** Motivated
Sometimes can focus away from T I'm responsible, so how do I get out of this?	Realises that body and mind need attention and sorting out	To let T show you what makes you feel better. To learn from T rather than fight it	**3** Resigned
Will it go? No responsibility. Everything and everyone else to blame. In denial	Tenuous link between restless mind and tense workhorse body	To accept responsibility. To open your mind to change. Can you carry on like this?	**2** Struggling
It will never go! No possibility of change. Total victim. Dependent	Lives in racing thoughts. Mind largely split off from body. Out of touch	To allow support in find hope and learn about getting better	**1** Stuck

© Cowan Hill 2015

Well-being Matrix for Tinnitus ©

Chapter 1 **Establishing the ground**

I had tinnitus moderately for 16 years, severely for 4 years and today I am not aware of it at all. When I get a cold, or overdo things, it sometimes creeps back as a feint fizzle, but that only takes up a few seconds of my attention. I feel very much that I have become cured of tinnitus and that I have learnt a lot about it through this process.

Like many of you, I was told there was nothing I could do about it and that I "had to learn to live with it," which came as a blow, to say the least. This is NOT true.

Anything that focuses your mind, distracts your attention away from tinnitus, and relaxes you will help this condition. There you are, three things that help already: FOCUSSING, DISTRACTION and RELAXATION. In this book you will find techniques that directly help you achieve these three goals, which help let go of tinnitus. As you practise them you will find out for yourself.

In this book you will follow the story of how I converted a maddening chorus of crickets in my head, chirping away all day and all night long, into a deep state of peace and stillness. You will receive mostly practical advice, techniques and key pieces of information that help take the power out of tinnitus and start it on its journey back into unawareness, where it came from.

I call these core pieces of advice "Core Issues." Please read them until you understand and know them thoroughly. Habitual patterns of thinking often take over our thought processes and can get in the way. You may quickly forget or "unknow" what you read here so I recommend revisiting these "Core Issues" a few times. They are taken from experience based working with hundreds of people over 8 years.

When you really understand what tinnitus is you will realise that my advice is common sense and that there really is a way out of this suffering. Here is the first piece of advice.

> **Core Issue 1: Negative People**
>
> Please let go of negative people who say there is nothing you can do about tinnitus. They are not going to help you. How can they honestly be of any use? The next time you hear someone say, "There's nothing you can do about it," shake their hands and say good-bye. Acknowledge that they are advertising the fact that they cannot help you. You need positive, constructive advice from people who understand this condition. They do exist. You have found one here.
>
> Unfortunately there are plenty of health practitioners that have little or no understanding of tinnitus. I meet plenty of people who have been given the wrong information and feel distressed as a result. What you don't need is to be exposed to tales of doom. It helps to be in touch with people who have learnt to let go of tinnitus themselves. Please know that tinnitus is not a fixed state. It can be changed and many people do get over this condition.

If you want to get better then you are going to need to understand what tinnitus is. The moment you understand what's going on and why you get it, this has two enormously positive effects:

Firstly, you will feel less threatened by it. This will help you calm down and start to let go. Working with tinnitus is all about letting go so that you can feel more confident and on top of things. To begin with, most people are scared of tinnitus because they haven't a clue what is going on and feel they have lost control. Understand it, and you will have taken a vital first step towards getting better.

Secondly, once you understand what tinnitus is, and how it works you will know how to manage it, and be better able to find the things that help. When you start looking after yourself properly, tinnitus starts getting better. When you realise this, you will feel relieved, much more in control and start relaxing. Anything that makes you relax, focus, and feel happy and comfortable helps tinnitus.

Chapter 1 – Establishing the ground

The moment you start improving you will become more motivated to take even more care of yourself. Taking more care of yourself helps symptoms back off further. This makes it easier to relax and let go more. The more you let go, the more tinnitus backs off. In fact it gets easier and easier the more progress you make. The most important stage is easing you out of stuck patterns of thinking. At the beginning we often get stuck in a negative cycle of thinking with tinnitus. There is a positive cycle too.

The next section is one of the most important parts of the book. I am going to explain what tinnitus is and why we get it. Please re-read this until you have got it. It took me a few months before I really understood what tinnitus was, and when the penny finally dropped I have been getting better pretty much ever since.

What is tinnitus?

Tinnitus comes when our nervous system goes into a state of red-alert. When we are too switched on, too sensitive, too wary, too on the look-out, all our senses become hypersensitive. In this state our hearing is so switched on that it not only picks up noise from the outside world, but also the sounds inside the body.

This is what tinnitus is: being so sensitive that you hear the internal noises as well as the external ones.

Your ears are listening out so intensely that you hear any sound inside your head. Nervous impulses along the acoustic pathways sound like hissing or high-pitched squeaks, movements of structures and fluids in the head create cracks and pops. A yawn, heartbeat or a click in the ear-tubes can sound like a deafening roar, a regular pulse or a bang, respectively.

Tinnitus means you are too switched on. This is a whole body thing and not just an ear thing. Your whole central nervous system is in red-alert and tinnitus is just one of the many side effects of this whole body reaction.

Many people are told tinnitus comes from damage to the hair-cells in the cochlea – the part of the hearing apparatus that detects sound. This is not true. Damage to the hair cells causes deafness, not tinnitus. When you become deaf, you strain to hear more. It is the straining to hear more that can temporarily increase your sensitivity. An increase in sensitivity can temporarily make you more prone to tinnitus, not damage to the hair cells.

Tinnitus needs your central nervous system, – that means your whole body, to be in a state of red-alert to exist. The state of your nervous system is very changeable. Going into a state of red-alert is a reversible process. We move in and out of it all the time.

The important point here is that this means tinnitus is reversible. The magic wand that helps undo tinnitus is to bring your central nervous system back out of a state of red-alert. This state is also known as: fight or flight, sympathetic nervous system arousal, hyperarousal, overwhelm, and the adrenal response. But in this book I will use the most instantly understandable term, red-alert.

Anything that brings you out of this state of red-alert will help your tinnitus.

Know that this state of red-alert is a temporary condition. When you come out of it your tinnitus will improve.

> **Core Issue 2: Tinnitus is NOT an ear-based problem**
>
> Stop thinking of tinnitus as coming from the ears. It is not your ears that are the Problem. The problem comes from the fact your whole central nervous system has become too switched on. To work with tinnitus you need to learn to get your whole central nervous system to switch off. This book shows you how to do this. It is far more useful to focus on working with your whole system rather than just the ears.
>
> Tinnitus is like a burglar-alarm. It is going off for a reason and is indicating that your nervous system still hasn't been able to switch off. The alarm is not the problem. You need to find out what triggered the alarm off in the first place. Trying to muffle the alarm or switch it off is not dealing with the problem and won't get rid of it.
>
> Tinnitus is a useful and healthy alarm that will quieten down when you start doing the right thing, start looking after yourself, and learn how to let go. The more your central nervous system settles and the more you feel well in yourself, the sooner the alarm will quieten.
>
> Stop blaming the alarm, and start dealing with what set it off. My aim is to help you enquire into what triggered the alarm off in the first place. As this becomes clear, you will know where you need to focus.

Many people tend to get very focused on specific things as THE single cause of their tinnitus, like a jaw problem, a knock on the head, or loud noise exposure. Of course these can trigger tinnitus, but they are likely to be the final straw that broke the camel's back, after a whole life-time of previous challenges.

I've met people who have pointed to a specific place just like a mechanic and said, "When this place is pressed, my tinnitus gets better, or if I hold my head like this, (they crane their neck to one side) then the sound subsides."

This is like a burglar-alarm going off and then trying to solve the problem by adjusting the position of the speaker, or fiddling about with the wiring. Of course interfering with the mechanism may have a big effect on the sound, but the cause of it still remains the same: your nervous system is TOO switched on.

The point here is that if you are not in a state to start off with, then you wouldn't still have the tinnitus now. Or to put this more clearly, a person who is really calm, centred and not in a state of red-alert, may get tinnitus from a blow to the head, but their tinnitus will soon subside. The fact that your tinnitus has not yet subsided is because you are still in a state of red-alert.

Most people get "normal tinnitus" after a loud concert or from exposure to silence. It pipes up and then goes away again. Continued tinnitus is there in the vast majority of cases because of a state of red-alert, and this state can change.

The trouble with focusing on one bit of your body or one event as a cause for tinnitus is that, you are still focusing on your tinnitus. If you want to keep your tinnitus going, then the best way to keep it there is to focus on it, worry about it, talk about it, and react against it. It doesn't matter if you are blaming a noisy drill, the next door neighbour, or a clicking jaw, what you are in fact doing is focusing on your tinnitus, homing in on your suffering and keeping it firmly there in your awareness.

Your reaction to your tinnitus, how you are relating to it right now is far more important in determining your progress than the event that triggered it.

If you are calm and happy inside, then the muscles won't be tight, the neighbours won't be irritating and the world won't wind you up. If you feel calm and happy inside, you are highly unlikely to spend much time noticing your tinnitus.

Secondly, remember that whatever you are blaming for your tinnitus is most likely to be the final straw after a long, and almost imperceptible layering of challenges onto your nervous system, called life.

A shockingly large percentage of the population over 50 have tinnitus. This is because as we get older we accumulate more experiences that have been overwhelming or hard to accept at the time. As a result we end up carting around this undigested life experience or "baggage" in our nervous system. There is more "stuff" that needs processing and this build up causes very specific reactions in our nervous system.

If you are 20 years old, and hit your head, you may get tinnitus for a day or two, but because your nervous system is relatively free and has enough available space to deal with challenging experiences, you get over things quickly. However, if you are 60, and you hit your head, you may get long-term tinnitus. This happens because you are much more likely to be bogged down with unprocessed baggage, resulting in overwhelm and a nervous system that goes into red-alert. Being in red-alert leaves you oversensitive and reactive. Therefore you notice the tinnitus more, create a reaction against it, and by so doing, lock it firmly into place in your awareness.

Older people are more prone to getting tinnitus not because of their age, but because they are less likely to have processed some of their baggage in therapy. You can start unpacking your "stuff" and lightening the load at any age. This will help you come out of red-alert.

It is not just one bit of your body, or one act that causes tinnitus, even though they are important. It is the prevailing general state of your central nervous system that leads to continued tinnitus. This means the way you approach yourself, the way you experience being in your body and how you treat yourself are central to what keeps tinnitus going!

Blaming the terrifying experience, bad news, operation, loud drill, medicine etc. is not taking the whole picture into account. You will have had a whole lifetime of challenges building up to that moment when the balance is tipped into a state of red-alert.

It is far more useful to focus on what makes you feel well in yourself and get guidance and support from a professional therapist. This will help you process a lifetime of experience held in you body, bring you out of a state of red-alert, and settle your system.

Merely focusing on releasing this muscle or repairing that bit of the body can be very frustrating as it is unlikely to lead you to the treasure at the end of the rainbow.

Chapter 2 What are tinnitus people like?

Recognising you are overwhelmed and getting support so that you can let go of this state is one of the most useful ways forward.

Before we look at how to come out of this state of red-alert, let's be really clear what we are talking about here. Red-alert has many tell-tale symptoms. How many of these can you recognise in yourself? Tick the ones that apply to you:

- Focussed in your head and not in your body
- Racing thoughts
- Tense body
- Not able to settle and switch off
- Can't do nothing – it's a waste of time!
- Constantly worrying
- Not able to feel body clearly
- Accelerated
- Never satisfied
- A driven approach to life
- Highly reactive to people around you
- Oversensitive to moods, atmospheres
- Always doing too much, working to lists, deadlines and achievements
- Easily angered, irritable
- Gets hot easily but hands and feet are cold
- Digestion is sensitive, bloated, irregular
- Forgetful
- Sleep is light and you wake easily

- Collapse in a heap at night, groggy in the morning
- Prone to anxiety and panic attacks
- Distracted by everything going on around
- Hard to focus on one thing
- Moody, up and down
- Crave sugary foods, coffee and other quick fixes
- Breathing is centred in upper chest rather than belly
- Breathing tends to be shallow and quick
- Eyes dart about
- Ears pick up all background noise
- Background noises are irritating and distracting
- Sensitive to smell
- Sensitive skin
- Heart beat is quick, too strong, accelerated or irregular

Don't worry if you have ticked quite a few of these. At this stage it is useful to start becoming aware of these patterns. Take a good look at yourself and observe what you are like.

The good news is that the moment you start coming out of this state of red-alert your ability to fight off disease improves, your digestion starts to work much more efficiently, your blood pressure becomes more regular, you sleep more deeply, your body relaxes, your mind slows down, you think more clearly, your memory improves, and your ability to be happy increases enormously. The point is, as you let go of tinnitus, your health transforms and the way you interact with the world changes on many levels.

Having worked with hundreds of tinnitus people, I have noticed how clear personality patterns emerge as well. Do any of these characteristics resonate with you?

- Give you a day off and you'll fill it with activity
- Quite critical of yourself and others
- Take on too much - can't say no.
- Have a point to prove
- Highly achievement orientated
- Need success and results
- Perfectionist that frets about the tiniest things
- Need to understand exactly what is going on
- Need to know why why why, and how
- Not the best listeners in the world
- Cerebral - lives in thoughts
- Meticulous
- Tell everyone about your problems
- Tendency to be highly strung
- Always things to do that need ticking off a list
- When you supposedly relax, you are still in your thoughts
- Tendency to blame people or external things as cause of your problems
- Look after everyone else but yourself
- Need to be heard, recognised, noticed, acknowledged
- Very good at doing, not good at just being

It doesn't matter if you have ticked some or all of these, the fact that you have tinnitus is a sign that something wants to switch off, and that something needs to let go.

Finally, before we start the process of how to get better, many tinnitus people need to find an answer to the question, "What caused it in the first place?"

The answer is: anything that overwhelmed you. Maybe you experienced something that was too exciting, too exhausting, too stimulating or just too much to digest or take in all at once. Here are some common examples of causes for tinnitus, although the list is endless:

- Exposure to loud noise
- Anaesthetics, surgery, operations
- Side effects of some medicines
- Overwhelming emotional situations
- Too much excitement
- Great fear
- Anger and frustration
- Overtiredness
- Too much change
- Too much responsibility
- Stress
- A blow to the head
- A bad cold/head based bug/virus
- Overstimulation
- Intense anger
- Long term worry e.g. court case, divorce, money problems
- Working overseas
- Long-haul flights, frequent jet-lag
- Exhaustion
- Syringing your ear

- Focussing on the ear
- Silence
- Jaw problems & major dentistry
- Lack of being looked after or supported
- Early mothering difficulties
- Being too compliant and not being allowed to say NO

Core Issue 3: Silence

Most people develop tinnitus if they are left in silence for too long. This may sound surprising but put anyone in silence and ask them to listen out for anything, then the majority will start hearing noises in their heads. Heller & Bergman (1953) carried out important studies that proved this. Why is this the case?

Our ears are happiest when they can rest with some noise going on in the background. When we are plunged into silence, this can sometimes activate a stress response and make us more acutely aware of our hearing. In the wild it is normal to hear background noise, but when things go quiet, it is normally before something dangerous. Our nervous systems know this!

So if silence brings on tinnitus, at the beginning it can be helpful to avoid silence or to create some background noise. This helps you to focus less on your tinnitus.

Hearing something agreeable in the background is a good idea while you still have this condition. In an ideal world you would live near a stream or fountain, or by the sea so that there is always something for your ears to relax onto. However try leaving a window open when you go to bed to let some noise in, or leave a laid-back CD or radio station on when you go to bed that switches itself off once you are asleep. The best is soothing, monotonous background music that is frankly a bit boring and that you won't pay too much attention to.

At first it seems really important to point the finger at someone or something for causing tinnitus. However I have learnt that most of the above are usually just the final straw that broke the camel's back, which tipped your system into overwhelm. Tinnitus people can be obsessed with the apparent thing that caused this condition to arise at the beginning, only to realise later that they were in a state anyway and something else would have come along and triggered it off.

When we are running on adrenaline in this state of red-alert, it is only a matter of time before something may act as a trigger. Please be wary of blaming certain situations for your tinnitus. If it hadn't been X it would have been something else soon after. It is your general state and reaction RIGHT NOW that is keeping the tinnitus going, not the original situation. That has long since gone. You need to deal with what you are left with in the present day, and how you are relating to this situation right now.

Core Issue 4: Stop trying to cure your tinnitus

I know this sounds strange, but I think this is a particularly important bit of advice. I have known people who make it their life mission to do everything in their power to stop the ringing in their ears. Great, you may think, until you consider that what they are in fact doing is focussing their whole life on their tinnitus. Focussing on tinnitus will keep it there in your awareness.

I have had clients to try hard to relax and then the first thing they do is check up to see if this has had any effect on symptoms. Of course you will do this out of habit at first. A normal part of being in red-alert mode is to check up and monitor everything all the time. If you go into every activity with a view to stopping tinnitus, then part of you will still be focusing on it.

To let go of tinnitus you need to take your focus off it, rather than reinforce it. I recommend focussing on brining well-being into your life rather than getting tinnitus out of it. Aim for things that make you feel good, comfortable and calm, with or without your tinnitus. The more you can bring in a sense of well-being with your tinnitus still there, the more it will feel manageable.

I always recommend putting tinnitus on the back shelf while you focus on developing a sense of well-being. Keep a clear intention to put all your energy into things that are nourishing, supportive, comforting, calming, and relaxing for your body.

Make your main focus getting your own needs met, finding things that make you feel happy and in touch with positive feelings. This approach works because it is much more attainable, gives you a sense of satisfaction and, most importantly, starts to bring you out of a state of red-alert.

The more you come out of this state of red-alert, the more you will create the conditions that allow tinnitus to back off.

Look for tinnitus and you will find it, look for comfort and relaxation and you will find that instead.

When tinnitus people start to realise the kind of care they need to give themselves, they often say, "Oh that's so selfish and self-indulgent. I have to look after my partner and my friends, or there is my business to consider. I have no time for all of this. I can't afford this."

In fact tinnitus people are brilliant at finding excuses to avoid looking after themselves. This is part of the make-up that has got them overwhelmed and in red-alert mode in the first place.

Well, the best thing you can do for your family and friends is be happy and well yourself. It may come as a blessed relief and take the pressure off everyone else! Most people have tinnitus because they do not have enough downtime or support, and simply don't look after themselves enough. They have to keep on doing doing doing doing, and have probably never been content with just being. I used to rush to get everything done so that I could relax. By the time I laid down I was in such a state that it took me half an hour to settle. These days I never rush, and take my time with everything. By the time I get to relax, I am already there.

The words "too much" and "not enough" are really important issues with tinnitus. What do you have too much of that burdens you and feels overwhelming, and what do you long for that you do not allow yourself? You probably know what I'm talking about. More time off, less responsibilities, more holidays, etc. Admit it to yourself. What is stopping you from saying No to the things you don't need and inviting in with open arms all the things that you know are nourishing and make you feel good?

Patterns such as these can be central to tinnitus because they set up a life-time of stress. Recognising and letting go of them can change things dramatically for the better. If you are struggling with issues like these then psychotherapy can really help you get to the core issues inside and help you find an happier and more appropriate way of being.

Most people also have a hard time accepting deeper issues like this because all they want is to turn the noise off NOW. There is a certain amount of impatience in the tinnitus personality. Please trust me with this, the moment you take positive action and do things that make you feel happy, well and relaxed, the sooner you will be able to make progress.

Most of you will think, "Yep, maybe he's right," and then do nothing absolutely about this. Beware of the part of you that sabotages all your plans to do anything helpful. Even when you understand how to stop it, which hopefully you will by the end of the booklet, a part of you will probably hold you back and say, "Wait a minute, I'm not doing this, because it won't work, its a waste of time, it won't work for me and so on." This part of you is called the Saboteur (See "Sacred Contracts" by Caroline Myss for details) and it will make sure that any progress is stopped in its tracks.

Most people with tinnitus have good intentions but are dominated with sabotaging thoughts like: how on earth will relaxing for half an hour every day help a problem like this?

Typical saboteur thoughts might be: What Julian describes here sounds like Nirvana and feels unobtainable. My uncle had it for 70 years so why should mine get better? My Doctor told me there was nothing I could do about it, and I believe him. It hasn't got any better yet, so why should it get better now? Thinking about my body is silly and how can this help something in my head?

Tinnitus people often are dogged by such thoughts. What helps is to recognise these thoughts when they pop up and then tell them to take a hike. If you want to get better you will probably come up against this part of you that is hell bent on staying miserable and stewing in it. I know this sounds extraordinary but we ALL have a saboteur inside.

> **Core Issue 5: Are you ready to change?**
> I am constantly amazed that people accept that they can develop tinnitus, moving from relative peace and quiet one day into a state of nerves and noise the next. But to suggest that they can change back out of that state where tinnitus backs off can be regarded like heresy. You can move into red-alert with no problems. Everyone can handle that. But to suggest you can revert back into peace mode for some is unthinkable.
>
> If you don't have tinnitus one year and then have it the next, why is it such a big deal to change again and be without it once more? You can change one way, so why is it so hard to change again? This is food for thought.
>
> The nervous system is a fluid, constantly altering state of balance. When the right conditions come along it changes.
>
> Please be wary of your own fixed thoughts and beliefs. What do you really think about this? Do you really think that you will have this for the rest of your life?
>
> How useful will it be for you to hold on to the belief that it will never go?
>
> Answer: it will be absolutely unhelpful in the extreme.
>
> Why on earth should you have this for the rest of your life? Things change all the time. Most people "habituate" to tinnitus, which means they eventually get

used to it, and their nervous system gets bored of checking up on it all the time. It no longer becomes such a big deal and therefore our awareness of it switches off. This is most likely to happen.

I know there are a lot of people out there who don't know much about this condition and say that there is nothing you can do, but please do yourself a favour and allow the possibility that you might just get better! There's nothing to lose and everything to gain by this change in belief pattern.

Of course its hard not to be infected by negative beliefs about tinnitus, especially when they come from health practitioners or people in authority. I can tell you not to listen to them and suggest you start sorting yourself out until the cows come home, but what really matters is what YOU really think inside? Be honest... Are you really prepared and ready to get better?

Its amazing how many people quite like certain aspects of tinnitus and don't want to let go of them. Believe it or not, I have met people that liked the attention it gave them. With tinnitus everybody became concerned about them and that extra attention was more important than getting better.

Strangely I have had a few clients that stopped coming for treatment the moment they started getting better. I sincerely believe that this was due to craving attention and being listened to by others.

Chapter 3   **How to make progress**

In the next section you will come to the **Well-being Matrix for Tinnitus** ©. This shows how people get better and outlines some of the general issues they have to work through to progress to a new level of improvement. I have put this together after years of study, work as a therapist with hundreds of people and of course direct personal experience and experimenting.

You will notice that I have divided the process of getting better into stages and have described how our relationship with tinnitus changes as we get better. For example, at the worst end of the chart people who are really struggling with this condition often feel like tinnitus has taken over their lives. I have described red-coloured level 1 as "stuck" and have described the way tinnitus behaves as a "tyrant."

However, as people get better and make progress they start to realise that tinnitus is actually a really useful healthometer that backs off when they do the right thing, and gets worse when they put themselves through stress, overexertion, anger etc. So up at yellow level, number 3 on the chart, I have described tinnitus as a doctor. Here, tinnitus shows you what is good for your health and you either take its advice and benefit, or fight against it and the tinnitus gets worse.

Eventually as you get much better, you no longer find yourself monitoring it anymore and it backs off for long periods of time. It may come back from time to time when you overdo things, but you know that it will quickly recede, because you look after yourself well enough not to react to it, or get into overwhelm. It really becomes no big deal if it reappears for a day or two because you know from experience that it backs off. At level 4 I have called tinnitus a "friend" as it is clearly a source of feedback that guides you reliably back to health.

The other columns of the **Well-being Matrix for Tinnitus** © highlight general patterns relating to people's states of awareness, thought patterns and challenges that they need to work through at each level. Please note, these are generalisations built on meeting many people and my intention here is to help you find yourself on your own particular path to progress. There will be many exceptions, and certain parts of the **Well-being Matrix for Tinnitus** © will overlap into different levels for different people.

My intention is to give you a framework for you to start doing the right thing, as well as to show you that letting go of tinnitus is not only possible, but also a well-trodden path. You are not alone.

We all know how difficult tinnitus can be, and I want to focus on getting better and how to let go of things. There is little value in focussing on doom and gloom.

Core Issue 6: Moaning and groaning

Some of you may have a tendency to complain to others about how awful your tinnitus is. You programme people with tales of your suffering until they automatically ask you every time they see you, "Oh hi there. How's your tinnitus?" You have a chat. Oh well, there's this negative thing... Oh and you would never imagine, that negative thing... Oh you can't possibly understand it. It's so negatively this, and negatively that, ... and old so-and-so struggled with it for 100 years... and before you know it you are feeling utterly depressed and even more focussed on it than ever. Please be aware that some tinnitus people are ingenious at focussing on suffering and building up a network that reinforces their suffering.

It is really important to get support and be able to express your feelings to others. But please be aware of a tendency to stew in one's own misery. This doesn't help.

I went to a tinnitus meeting once, which turned into a competition to see who was suffering the most.

Oh hi, how are you?

> Terrible thanks. It's been driving me mad this last week.
>
> Oh me too. Is there ever going to be an end to this?
>
> I don't know. I know someone who did X, and experienced Y, and then they felt terrible.
>
> Oh that's terrible.
>
> And then they went to so-and-so for help who was terrible, and then they felt even more terrible.
>
> God that's really terrible, that is.
>
> They had it for a hundred and ninety-seven years. Isn't that terrible.
>
> God I feel terrible now.
>
> So do I…
>
> It is so important to have support with tinnitus and feel you are properly listened to and understood, but please beware of the "terrible sessions." I personally didn't find them useful. Joining a group of moaners can be very draining and counter-productive.

You need to surround yourself with people who:

- Can teach you how to let go mentally, emotionally and physically
- Help your body feel calm and comfortable
- Can listen to you and help you process your feelings about it

- Care about your well-being
- Make you happy, laugh and enjoy yourself
- Help you focus, become clear
- Inspire you
- Bring other interests into your life
- Take your mind off tinnitus

If you can find people who:

- Are positive about tinnitus
- Understand what you are going through
- Understand tinnitus and how it works

then that is great. Treasure them!

Core Issue 7: Avoiding doom and gloom

As long as tinnitus still bugs you, please be vary careful of doom and gloom out there in the world. Stop watching the news and horror films if you can. Seeing and hearing traumatic events in other peoples lives is traumatising in itself. We get addicted to the adrenaline rush that this creates and locked into dark misery facing the world. This is highly activating and tends to move us towards a state of red-alert.

When the news comes on, turn over. When Mr & Mrs Grim turn up at the door, pretend you are out. If there is nothing but horror films and depressing documentaries on TV, go to the cinema and see a comedy instead!

Do yourself a favour and protect yourself from this daily challenge to your nervous system. When you are feeling better you will be able to cope with this, but just for now, it may well help to steer clear of doom and gloom. No more waking up to the radio full of stories about war, famine and death. You need light, comic, gentle, relaxing, digestible and uplifting input. Leave saving the world until you are really feeling strong again.

> ### Core Issue 8: Don't let vampires sap your energy
> We all know people who are energy drains. You meet up for a chat and after ten minutes you feel exhausted. Next time they get in touch, take a rain check and agree to meet them next year. You need all the energy you can get just now, and cannot afford to support everyone else's needs if your tinnitus is bad. Not today Mr and Mrs Vampire! Go and find someone else to sap.
>
> When we are in red-alert mode we are running on adrenaline. This is our emergency energy supply, so if we stay in this state for a long time we eventually get exhausted. Tinnitus thrives on exhaustion.
>
> What really helps let go of tinnitus is to build up a steady energy supply that is there for you and you only. Say good-bye to the vampires. Tell them to get a therapist!

Running on adrenaline is a bit like taking out an energy overdraft. Rather than using energy that is available and there for you to use on a daily basis, in red-alert mode you start using up your emergency energy reserves. Your energy level has already run out. The more you dip into adrenal energy, the sooner you will burn out. Eventually you will have to pay it back. This is experienced in the body as symptoms that get louder and louder the more you ignore them.

To pay back your energy overdraft you need time off, a healthy diet, regular exercise, daily downtime just for yourself. You need to build space into your life. Siestas and naps can really help pay off the sleep deficit. If you are overtired, sleeping often helps you to sleep more. Most people try and keep going without sleep till bed-time and because they are exhausted, cannot sleep properly. A short siesta after lunch works wonders and seems to be ultra refreshing and regenerating. For exhausted nervous systems it seems **the more you sleep, the more you can sleep**.

Core Issue 9: Letting go into support

If tinnitus is all about letting go, then you need to build up a support network around you to let go into. You can't let go into nothing. It is so much harder to let go by yourself. Once you find the right kind of support, then you can start to let go in earnest. This is a process which takes time, and slowly, important changes start to take place. To put it another way, all the important changes tend to happen slowly over a period of time. Quick fixes bring short-term relief, which is great, but nonetheless, are still short-term.

This is where therapy comes in. The ideal would be to find a body-based therapy like craniosacral therapy, massage, reflexology or acupuncture, and balance this with a mental-emotional support like psychotherapy, or counselling. The moment you start bringing support in, the pressure will start to ease off and the process of letting go will happen all by itself. Take a mid-long term view if you can with therapy.

I was lucky to come across craniosacral therapy with a gentle and sensitive approach that works at the physical, mental, emotional and energetic level. For more details go to www.craniosacral.co.uk. I recommend it highly.

I also recommend Core Process Psychotherapy developed by the Karuna Institute in Devon. www.karuna-institute.co.uk/. This work helps us get in touch with our deepest issues and helps find a way out of suffering that touches into Buddhist Wisdom.

I really encourage you to find an approach that suits you. Once you have a support network in place, this will allow you to gradually open up, process your issues, and start to let go. This is what brings you out of red-alert mode. It is much harder doing this by yourself. Let's face it, how able are you to let go just now? You probably have tinnitus right now because there is something you cannot let go of.

Get support so that you can start letting go is the simplest and most powerful piece of advice in this book.

Having professional therapeutic support from someone neutral rather than your partner or friend makes a huge difference. The safe, confidential environment and careful interaction will most likely help you relax and let go far more than you are used to.

My advice here is to find someone you feel comfortable with, and then build up a long-term therapeutic relationship with them. These people are trained to look after you and gradually you will notice how you find things become more manageable. This is not a quick fix. You have a whole lifetime of experience in your body and this will need proper support that develops over a period of time.

It really helps to be open with your practitioner about any worries you have. Please, if you are struggling with something, or are not happy with any part of this process, do speak to them about it. Very often when we want to run away or when we come across areas of difficulty, this can be very revealing and helpful to work through. All too often people just stop going, and flit from one thing to the next, never really being able to work through the important things, and never being able to let go.

You can find details of practitioners at your local health food shop, the library and on the internet. If you want a professional referral then contact the association of the therapy you are interested in and then ask for a practitioner from the register. Most therapies have a website with registered practitioners' details available.

I personally couldn't have let go of tinnitus alone. Professional help and support has allowed me to transform as a person, becoming happy, relaxed and clear-headed.

It takes a great deal to ruffle me these days, and I have a sense of continuing to get stronger and stronger.

Five years ago a mere cup of coffee would heighten my tinnitus, whereas my system is strong enough to drink it every day with no side effects. This is the same for tea, alcohol and chocolate. Stimulants may have the same effect on you, and equally they may not. However, if they do, you need to listen to the best doctor you have, that is your body's reactions. If your tinnitus pipes up after drinking too much coffee or alcohol, then you know what you need to do.

Core Issue 10: Diet

Eating a healthy diet that suits your system, and cutting down on stimulants will take the pressure off your nervous system. The less your system has to struggle with toxins and foods that don't agree with you, the more it can switch off.

My tinnitus really improved when I gave up sugar, wheat and fermented or processed foods. I'm not suggesting you should give up wheat or fermented food, but you may find that certain foods make you feel much calmer and more comfortable. There are plenty of books that outline certain kinds of food that are settling for your system. See a qualified nutritionist if you suspect any digestive difficulties and find dietary advice in your bookshop.

The best advice is let your body tell you. If you eat well you will feel well. If you suspect something is bad for you, then give it up for a couple of weeks, and then reintroduce it, and notice the difference. There is nothing clearer than your body's reaction to diet.

Giving up sugar is incredibly positive for the body. If you eat very sugary food your body has to work very hard to bring the blood sugar levels back into check. Your pulse goes up because this triggers a mild adrenal response activating the red-alert state a little (as does caffeine). This can have implications for tinnitus, just as anything else that creates resistance and a struggle in your system.

For some people cutting back on stimulants can make a difference. Try Red Bush tea instead of normal tea. It's the closest alternative to normal tea that is equally refreshing but you can drink gallons of it and it is good for you.

Core Issue 11: Exercise

Having regular gentle exercise is hugely helpful. This not only helps take your mind off tinnitus and stops you "stewing in it", but also helps your body release and let go of tension and toxins. Gentle exercise is an excellent way of getting in touch with your body and letting go. Remember working with tinnitus is all about letting go.

Rather than going at it hammer and tongs, I recommend little and often is a less stressful way for your system. When my symptoms were bad I went swimming most days for just 10 minutes. I built up my fitness gradually over a period of time, and found that I always felt better for the contact with water.

It is very hard to worry about tinnitus or even focus on it when you are enjoying the feeling of floating and moving through water.

I feel that a long-gentle walk is better than a hard game of squash or an exhausting weight-lifting session. Low-impact, frequent and enjoyable exercise is the best.

Once again, you need to find what suits you. If you feel tired and lousy and decide to do some tough exercise, find you get onto a high, only to crash half an hour later, then you are probably pushing yourself a bit too hard. Work gradually into exercise at a level which suits you. Your tinnitus will probably let you know what's best.

Find some exercise that you enjoy and leaves you feeling calm, comfortable, in touch with your body, but not exhausted.

> **Core Issue 12: Getting in touch with your body**
>
> Learn to become aware of your body. Body based therapies will help you become much more grounded, which means aware of how you feel inside. When I had bad tinnitus, I would often feel out of touch with the felt sense of my body. In fact my awareness would often be elsewhere, far off in my though processes and very out of touch with the here and now.
>
> There is one thing that is always grounded in the here and now, and that is your body. The more you get in touch with how it feels, the more you will know what is good for you, what your true feelings are about things, and the more you will be in touch with your energy.
>
> Focussing on the body directly helps you get in touch with reality, helps your nervous system get its bearings, and amazingly, helps you switch off and let go.
>
> One of the biggest problems with letting go is not knowing what you need to let go of. **You cannot let go of what you don't know**. If you learn to get in touch with how you feel inside, letting go will become much clearer and more possible.
>
> Bringing my awareness into the body is the one thing that helped me let go of my tinnitus more than anything else.

When I was in tinnitus mode, a walk across town was spent almost entirely deep in thought. I was constantly chasing thoughts about and worrying about imaginary events that would never take place. I was totally unaware of how my body felt as I walked past people, and spent very little attention just seeing what was there and hearing the sounds about me. My senses were totally taken over by my mind. A walk across the woods was spent planning the next week, or having an imaginary argument with a difficult person.

These days I notice what is going on in the present moment, smell the smells, see what is there, and feel my body expanding with pleasure when I experience something I like, and shrink and judder when I am exposed to something unpleasant. The biggest difference is that I am not locked away in some imaginary land of thoughts, putting me out of touch with the moment. Instead I am there, experiencing the world through my body and the felt sense of it. I am more present and in touch with all of me and not just my head. Tinnitus really hates this.

When I meet someone I can feel my body opening up or pulling away from them, regardless of what I think or what is going through my mind. I can feel my own energy as a force field in and around me and instantly notice when I am being drained or inspired.

It is such a relief not to live in thought processes all the time. My body is there in my awareness when I am talking to someone, watching TV, and going off to sleep. Life seems much more real and I feel much calmer and happier from this more embodied perspective.

Where are you focused? How often are you aware of your body when you are engaged in some activity? Can you feel your body as you are reading this text just now? A lot of tinnitus people spend a lot of time with their awareness not in their body.

Most of the techniques in this book help you to become embodied. As you practice being aware of how your body is, your mind will start to take root more and more in your body so that you can rest there. Lean to live through your body and tinnitus will not like it one bit!

Chapter 4 **Charting your progress**

So now that we have got some of the ground-work in place, lets start the process of getting better.

Please look at the **Well-being Matrix for Tinnitus** © at the beginning of the book. I suggest you take a copy and place it somewhere where you will notice it.

This matrix charts how people get better, showing the landmarks of progress along the way in seven levels. When you notice how you are improving, this is really encouraging and can help spur you on your way to the next level. By sharing the pitfalls and challenges that I and many of my clients have struggled with along this journey to recovery, my aim is to stop you from making the same mistakes! I also would like to comfort and reassure you that you are not alone, and that getting better is a well-trodden path. If you follow the guidelines set out over the next seven levels in the book, and learn from where we have got stuck, you will be in a much better position to make progress yourself.

Learning how to look after yourself properly and becoming aware of how you treat yourself and your symptoms is crucial for making progress. When you look after yourself appropriately you will get better. Part of the challenge is learning what works specifically for you and getting your own needs met. We are all different and need different things to bring in a sense of well-being.

Let's look into each stage and help you find where you are on your path to letting go of tinnitus.

Level 1: **Stuck**

The red level of the matrix is called STUCK. People here are under the illusion that there is no way out and that the tinnitus will never go. It is common to sink into this mindset when we have been misinformed by a health practitioner that there is nothing we can do about it. It is not surprising that we give up hope if the person we go to for help gives us this message of negativity. Once again, please ignore such messages. They are totally unhelpful. I strongly advise steering clear of such people.

At this level of suffering you often feel totally at the mercy of tinnitus, which can behave like a TYRANT. You are afraid of losing control and feel powerless to stop it. Although this is the way it seems, this is most definitely not the case. When you are deeply locked into a state of red-alert, it is normal to feel hunted, anxious, fearful and as if there is no hope. This is normal behaviour for red-alert mode.

But there is hope. Look up the matrix to the next levels and see what it's like for people who have improved. As you get to know this matrix better by going through your own process of starting to look after your own needs more, you will recognise some of the landmarks of change in your awareness. As you improve you will be able to keep track of changes in the way you relate to tinnitus, think about it and feel in yourself.

At level 1 you may notice that you live almost entirely in your head, stuck in racing thoughts. Your days are filled with interminable mental chit-chat that seems to dominate everything. These thoughts can often be negative and full of worry. Do you have a sense of being locked inside your head just now? How easy is it to describe what is going on inside your body, or how things feel sitting here reading this? Of course you will be thinking about what you are reading, but as I write this, I can feel my bottom clearly sitting on the chair and my legs feel really calm and comfortable.

See if you can get a sense of where you are focussed just now. Does it seem like the centre of attention is in your head? If your body is like a house, are you upstairs in the attic, or do you have a clear sense of how your lower body is downstairs? Where is your focus just now? How able are you to describe what is going on in your body?

Chapter 4 – Charting your progress

When we are in red-alert we tend to spiral in our thoughts and sometimes feel like we are spaced out and floaty. If there is a focus it might feel generally around the head area, but distinctly floaty. Do you feel floaty from time to time?

It is very common for tinnitus people to be almost entirely out of touch with their bodies. If you ask them how they feel, they will often be unaware of anything below the neck, other than tightness and aches and pains. Most of you will probably fall into this category.

This is why having comforting, soothing, relaxing body-work is so important. Feeling the direct contact of warm, caring hands that know what they are doing will calm the system down, and will help you feel how your body is. As soon as the body relaxes, your mind stops racing and starts slowing down, and you start feeling a little bit more in touch with what feels okay.

For me having hands-on body work was an absolute Godsend when my tinnitus was bad. My body started to experience calm, safe and comforting experiences which directly helped my nervous system shift down out of red-alert mode. It helped much more than I realised at the time. Please do yourself a huge favour, find a good therapist and have regular body-work. Once a week for a few months should really help you get in touch.

Your mind will probably say: "Oh this won't help. How is this going to stop my tinnitus? I want it to stop right NOW! My tinnitus hasn't gone yet. Oh this person doesn't understand what it is like. I need pills and a quick fix rather than all this alternative stuff. I've had three massages and my tinnitus hasn't got any better. This is useless. Nobody can help me. This will never go." When you find the saboteur taking over your mind and trying to sabotage any plans to help yourself, take it from me that this will help and tell the saboteur to be quiet!

Acknowledge that you do actually want to get better, rather than stew in all this misery. Know that looking after how you feel on any level and getting your needs met will help. Until you actually try this out, you will have to trust me. Get support and start experiencing the changes. Just staying in your head and reading this from a mental point of view is barely going to scratch the surface.

We all have a tendency to sabotage things we know are good for ourselves, especially when we are down at this level. How do you think we got here in the first place?

Being in touch with your body really helps. The more you can focus on how your body feels, the more you can take your mind off tinnitus. Craniosacral therapy worked incredibly well for me. I was continually surprised by how I thought I was relaxed and then suddenly, something would let go and I would sink into a delicious state of calm. Then, after a period of time, I would drop into a whole new level of calm and comfort that I frankly had never known before. Relaxing is relative and seems to get endlessly better. Just when you think you are relaxed, with help, bodywork and support, you suddenly relax a hundred times more. One thing is critical in being able to relax, your body needs your attention. Having someone working on your body helps gather your awareness into your body space, and this leads to relaxation.

At level 1 it's great that you are already reading this, which is a step in the right direction. Read through this booklet until you understand it thoroughly. It will be a support in itself. It is my intention to inspire you to learn how to look after yourself and to give you hope and a sense of motivation. I was at rock bottom and struggled with tinnitus for years. Now I have never been so well. Please know that this is possible.

In my clinic, clients who experience six sessions or so find things starting to feel much more manageable. Tinnitus no longer bugs them so much and they are able to focus more clearly on what makes them feel better. Those that follow the advice in this book and practice focusing on how their bodies feel make very good progress.

To get out of STUCK and start moving up a level it is really important to get regular therapy for your body and mind. Remember, letting go only really becomes possible when you have support. It is so much easier when you can offload onto someone. When this person is neutral and has no strings attached, and when this support is on a regular basis, it is hard not to feel some benefit. You have to be pretty determined to be miserable to not start feeling some relief.

Know that as soon as you start creating a neutral space where you can process how you feel inside, you will start unburdening your issues and setting out on the road to letting go. Find someone you feel comfortable with and allow yourself to really unburden yourself and offload onto them. That's what they are paid for.

Tinnitus people are champions of trying things out just once, and then saying it was useless and moving on to something else. Please be aware of flitting from one thing to the next and never really getting anywhere. I now refuse to treat people with tinnitus who won't commit to at least six sessions. This usually ensures that they not only do they get onto the right track and gain a sense of direction, but also usually start feeling much better. This motivates them to keep progressing up the matrix to a level where they feel satisfied. Those who come for just a couple of sessions tend to just stay stuck.

Some of you may feel there is nothing wrong with you. My advice is to go to body-work and start to find out how you really feel inside. You have tinnitus. That is a good enough reason to get help.

As I have already mentioned, it is not helpful to try to stop your tinnitus at this level. Don't aim to climb the final ascent of Everest before you have all your sherpas and supplies in order. That is a long way off just now. Keep your aims within reach and realistic. Just now, try to aim for anything that makes your body feel more relaxed and comfortable, and allows you to have a good cry, release emotions and clear your head. What really helps is to find someone who can really LISTEN to you, and get a sense of what you are going through. Trained therapists are best for this.

Trying to stop your tinnitus is just another way of focussing on it. You need to take the focus away from it just now.

Put your tinnitus on the back shelf, even if it is howling. Make your focus and main aim anything that makes you feel well. It doesn't matter if it is lying in a jacuzzi for an hour every day, or hanging upside down from the rafters, turn yourself into a student of well-being who experiences increasingly long periods of calm, relaxing, manageable, and happy activities. This helps tinnitus. Pushing yourself to the limit doesn't.

If you have children to look after or tough business commitments, organise some down time on a regular basis. If this is seemingly impossible you really need to consider whether your lifestyle really suits you. Tinnitus people often drive themselves into overwhelm where the need for money, power, and achievement seems to outweigh well-being. Your body is one reality you have to deal with. If you want to let go of tinnitus, something has to give. As you build up more of a support network, things will become more manageable and well-being will return.

The power of direct contact from someone who is calm and happy is extraordinary. At this level I feel it is essential. However it also really helps to build up your positive resources. By that I mean all the things that make you feel well.

What really helped me through the difficult days were: lying in a jacuzzi, swimming, taking the dog for a walk, laughing, having a long shower working the jet all along my spine, having a good cry, spending time with happy, positive people, not talking about my tinnitus and dwelling on it all the time with everyone I met, avoiding depressing and draining people, letting go of all the stressful things in my life, turning the news over to a comedy show, having long baths with lavender and candlelight, the smell of roses and putting rose oil on my pillow, listening to gentle, beautiful music, spending long periods of time just doing nothing, talking to someone who cared about my well-being, lying in the sun, swinging in a hammock at the bottom of the garden, lying in the middle of the floor in the middle of the living room in the middle of the day doing nothing, daydreaming about happy memories, beautiful places, laughing a bit more, getting into delicious, healthy cooking, taking up photography, learning how to use the computer, going on holiday, learning salsa, Scottish dancing, going to the cinema and watching uplifting, happy, slow-paced films, reading endless inspiring books, pottery, wine-tasting, learning languages, all these things really helped me. It took the focus away from tinnitus, made me feel happier, put me in contact with others and helped me relax.

To be honest, this list of things that make me feel happy was much shorter to start off with when my tinnitus was bad. Of course it was. I was out of touch with all the things I loved in life and that was part of the problem. But the more I took care of myself, the longer this list got, and the better I felt and the more my tinnitus backed off.

What are your resources? What makes you happy, inspired, relaxed, hopeful, comfortable? How much downtime do you have and how much enjoyment do you let into your life? The core issue here is how loving and kind you are to yourselvef. We tinnitus people tend to treat ourselves like tyrants, bossing ourselves around, pushing hard and being pretty unforgiving and demanding at the best of times. Learning to treat ourselves well is tantamount to being loving and kind to ourselves.

It is really essential for you to start allowing all the good things into your life that you need to be well. Start looking after yourself and letting in all the things you long for. Be kind and loving to yourself like you would be to a child, and stop pushing, demanding and expecting so much of yourself. Give yourself a break. You need to know what helps you, what makes you happy. As soon as you become aware of this and start allowing what you long for into your lives, your tinnitus will show you that you are on the right path and back off.

Many people with tinnitus say that they have jobs, families and responsibilities they cannot get out of, leaving them with no time to themselves. The issue is more likely not being able to say no, or not setting clear boundaries and asking to be left alone. If we are honest, the best thing for our families and businesses is to be well and happy. The more we look after ourselves, the more we can bring to our relationships at home and at work.

It is all about letting go. We need support and positive resources to nourish us over a period of time in order to let go. Please give yourself plenty of time.

At this level I strongly advise weekly therapy/counselling/bodywork sessions. Don't expect miracles to start off with. This is not a quick fix, although some people experience great improvement at the beginning, and that can be such a relief. My advice is to keep going with your sessions.

Most of all you will want your tinnitus to get better right now, but please be patient and try to keep your goals manageable. Aim for any kind of well-being just now. You will be able to deal with tinnitus more directly once you have established a positive support network and have moved up a level. At this stage it is good enough to get some sense of well-being. Get your sherpas and supplies in order first, before starting the ascent. Build up your positive resources and give yourself a bit of time to establish this.

Can you write a list of all the things that make you feel better? What nourishes you and makes you relax?

I thoroughly recommend joining a regular tai chi, yoga, relaxation, Pilates, or Alexander Technique class. With the support of a teacher and people around you, this will help enormously. Once again you can find out about this on the internet, at the library, and in health food shops. Do a whole course before you consider if it is for you or not. Give it a chance to work.

> ### *Technique 1: Crisis calmer*
> *When you get into a state, try immersing your feet into a bowl of comfortably hot water for fifteen seconds, and then plunge them into a bowl of cold water. Move them backwards and forwards from hot to cold, back and forth for a good ten minutes. Notice how your focus settles more into your body. This simple technique is great for calming you down, getting you out of your head and slowing down any panicking thoughts. In more distraught moments, this will help take the pressure off, and will help divert your attention away from your head. Try it and feel for yourself.*

Level 2: **Struggling**

When we start getting help, this can be a really interesting time. I found myself coming out of what felt like a numbed down state, and I started to get in touch with how I felt emotionally, physically and mentally. I discovered that I was full of anger and frustration, and that my body was holding onto lots of "baggage."

BUT I was finally telling my story to someone. I was being listened to and supported and I found myself starting to off-load and process a great dam of stuff I hadn't realised was there. It was difficult at times, but it felt like something was shifting. Even though sessions could be quite challenging I started to feel lighter and like I was relaxing and letting go. Over a period of time I became noticeably more comfortable going to someone for help, and opening up to them. I had no idea how much stuff had become pent up inside.

Level two is all about struggling with tinnitus. It is like having a sergeant major that has moved in with you, orders you about and has you on a short leash.

Being listened to carefully is particularly important for people at this stage. You may find yourself blaming the diving accident, the syringe, the loud drill, the medication, the cold and a whole host of people, events and situations. It may seem like they all caused your tinnitus and it had nothing to do with you! Therapy may help you realise otherwise.

This is the level where you get endless worrying thoughts swooping down into your mind like vultures: "If I hadn't done X, then the tinnitus wouldn't have appeared. That wretched so-and-so. I was fine before they did Y to me." This is the classic time for pointing the finger at noisy neighbours, inconsiderate partners, and nasty health practitioners who just make it worse. You may find yourself really giving yourself a hard time, and well, frankly beating yourself up with thoughts like: "I cannot accept this. I used to be in control. I want my peace back. I don't want to have to look after myself any differently or do bloody relaxation exercises. No no no!"

Get it off your chest. Let it all out. Once you have the support of a therapist then its great just to be honest and share your feelings. You can really start to notice just what you are like. For tinnitus it is best to be calm and in a settled state, but you most probably got into this state in the first place because of bottled up feelings. They will need to come out, in order for you to let go. With a good therapist, this process can be handled carefully, slowly and feel manageable. Keeping the brakes on slightly is much more healing than flying headfirst into overwhelming process.

Many people go through the, "Why me? Why should I look after myself? I should be well. There's nothing wrong with me!" stage. In order for this to happen, you need someone there to express this to, ie a therapist.

It's no good unleashing all this to your partner or nearest and dearest. That will just bring them down too leaving you all feeling full of doom and gloom, depleted and at the end of your tether. A therapist can be a much more powerful support because they are neutral and have no strings attached. Although they are affected by what you bring into the space, they have the means to not be overwhelmed by you and remain strong. This brings much more space to this densely packed baggage we all carry, and allows us to process and air it in a safe transformational way.

In STRUGGLING, the mindset is already different to level 1. The fact that you are prepared to do something about it means that you are considering the possibility that your tinnitus may get better. Here people are starting to question their symptoms and are wondering if it really will be there forever, or perhaps, maybe it might just get a little bit better.

You may find that when you get in touch with anger or anxiety during sessions your tinnitus may react and flare up. But believe me it is worth getting things off your chest because this is what allows you to settle later. While I was struggling through the first stages of getting better, sometimes I would go through a shift and then my tinnitus would wobble and react for a few days afterwards.

I constantly get asked by people at this level, "Will it make my tinnitus worse?" The honest answer is temporarily we can get slight aggravations, but fortunately most of the time the nervous system settles and you just feel calmer. When tinnitus flares up after a session, this is often because something is changing and being processed by your system and usually you have a sense of this feeling quite important and appropriate, even if you feel a bit emotional or jangled for a day or two. But after each flare up, things settle to a slightly easier level in my experience, and over a period of time the overall trend is positive.

I can remember feeling really shocked when I suddenly realised that nobody in my family ever truly listened to me. Of course from day to day we all used to talk to each other, but nobody ever really considered my needs because they all had such strong agendas themselves. We were all bogged down and so none of us could be there for each other.

I became aware of how I had shut down and just gone numb as a defence. Even though this was challenging to come to terms with at the time, this realisation marked a turning point in my own journey of getting my own needs met. For the first time these needs were being met deeply, and I was being heard and attended to. The sense of relief was extraordinary.

I can't help but feel how common this is with tinnitus people, the need to be heard and acknowledged. So much of this condition is about needing other people to know how bad it is, and for them to really listen to this and hear you. How often do we get really frustrated that nobody seems to be taking us seriously or that they don't understand what it is like?

Practically every client of mine says at some stage, "Well Julian, at least you have been through this and know what it is like. That is such a relief to me, and one of the main reasons I have come to see you."

At this level it is also common to be strongly in denial. You may be thinking that you are very together and that you don't need therapy. Please remember that if you are really well and have no burning issues and have digested and processed all your life experiences thoroughly, then you should be able to let go of tinnitus quite quickly. If you have tinnitus that won't go away, this is a sign that something needs to let go.

You can probably remember noticing tinnitus when you were a teenager as your head hit the pillow after a loud concert, only to find that it had disappeared by morning. However, if your tinnitus is still there, the fact that you are holding on to it is a sign that something needs to shift.

The only exceptions to this are being deaf or partially deaf, which causes you to strain to hear. This heightens your sensitivity, which can lead to tinnitus. Because you don't hear well, your nervous system becomes ultra sensitive so it can pick up more information from outside world. By straining in this way, you end up picking up internal noise as tinnitus.

Alternatively there is an extremely rare medical condition that can lead to tinnitus called an acoustic neuroma. Sometimes people are sent off for a brain scan, even though the odds are remote. I'm always amazed how many people are put through this procedure. How often are we sent off for a brain scan when we have headaches? It almost seems as if health practitioners send people off for a scan because they don't know how else to deal with tinnitus. The tinnitus person, being in an anxious state is bound to rise to the suggestion that there is a slim chance they have this or that, and therefore feel they should get it checked out. But if they get stressed out by the process, then their tinnitus may get worse as a result. How much are scans of this type about pandering to anxiety rather than seriously managing someone's well-being?

The point is that the vast majority of tinnitus cases come from being in a state of red-alert and this can change. If you are prepared to go through the hassle of taking the brain scan route, then please also consider setting up a support network and establish a therapeutic relationship too. This is more likely to help you settle into a state where you can let go of tinnitus.

At level 2 tinnitus can be really frustrating. It can flare up at the slightest thing. Even relaxing can create this extraordinary paradox where you are much more centred and aware of how you are and, as a result, you notice it more. You feel better and clearer, but as all the chaos and turmoil starts to subside you may notice the tinnitus more.

I can remember, as all of my frantic thought processes started to calm down, a clearer head meant I became more aware of tinnitus as a result. As the storm clears the cause of irritation sticks out more. This can be challenging. But you have to ask yourself which is better: being lost in a sea of chaotic thought and distractions that drown out the tinnitus, or being calm and clear and able to notice the tinnitus in all its glory?

Even though tinnitus can stick out like a sore thumb at times when you feel particularly calm and peaceful, these moments are crucially important. You start to really meet tinnitus full on, face to face as it were. At times it seems we need to be able to fully experience our tinnitus and learn to be well with it at the same time, before it starts backing off. How you react now is going to become a deciding force in what happens next. You can either react negatively and wind yourself up, or what I suggest is that you try the techniques at the end of this level. As you become more able to meet tinnitus in a much more direct, head-on kind of way, get into a regular habit of practising a well-being inducing technique. The more you do this, the more your subconscious will start associating tinnitus with a reason to relax and be well, and the less threatening it will become.

The technique at the end of this section is one of the most useful in the whole book. Whereas once I used this to let go of tinnitus, now that I no longer have this problem, I continually depend on clenching and relaxing to settle myself down. It helps enormously when life gets challenging, when I am angry, in pain, confused or exhausted. Learning to focus on the body can really transform our experience of difficulty.

A word of advice about having a really relaxing therapy session: If you find that after a treatment you really let go, switch off and start noticing your tinnitus more, it can be tempting to blame the person who helped you. You may need to go through a period of noticing how you are in all your glory, good and bad, and for some people the bad parts eg tinnitus, being negative, impatient, destructive, critical, driven, pushy etc can be hard to accept. My advice is to keep on going with therapy and focus on the increasing sense of well-being in your body. Just keep going. Some people give up at this stage which is such a shame as they are only just starting to do the work. You may have to really pamper yourself for the time being while you struggle through this challenging stage. But learning what helps is a vital part of the process.

As you start getting in touch with how you feel inside, you may start noticing how achy, tired, tense and painful your body is. Many people with tinnitus treat their bodies like workhorses and don't really look after them much. Even though it is uncomfortable getting in touch with this, I encourage you to work through things with a body worker to help release some of this tension. It does get easier with time but getting in touch with difficult is some of the most important work you will do on yourself. This is where you make progress. This is also why you need the support of a therapist. Level two can really seem like a place of "no pain, no gain" at times.

You may come across feelings you didn't know were there. Use the support of your therapist to help process any issues that arise. They are trained to help you in this way.

The challenge of this level is to really start considering how you can bring changes into your lifestyle and how you approach your body and mind. If you start therapy and bring extra support into your life, this is an enormous step in the right direction and that alone with a month or two is very likely to move you up a level or two on the scale.

In the meantime, be good to yourself. Don't push yourself to the limit. Bullying yourself, driving yourself to exhaustion, or taking on too much are definitely things that you need to seriously consider stopping. Bring in enough down-time, and allow as much fun and humour flood into your life as possible. Stop taking yourself so seriously and let yourself just be as you are.

Who is really the sergeant major here – the tinnitus or you? Is the tinnitus really to blame or is it just your body reacting to the way you treat yourself?

One of the most useful things you can do at this level is start to notice how well you treat yourself. When was the last time you gave yourself a proper break? How much downtime do you have on a daily basis? What do you do on a regular basis that makes you feel happy, calm and focussed? How much support do you have around you? The message you need to take on board here is that you need to start taking good care of yourself, and giving yourself time to become aware of how you really feel inside. Here is a really useful technique that puts you in touch with how you are. The more aware you become of how you are inside, the easier it becomes to let go of it. Remember, we can't let go of what we don't know. So, get to your what's going on inside.

Technique 2: Clenching and relaxing

Stop thinking and start feeling! This exercise allows you to really get in touch with your body and find out what it needs. Learn to feel how your body is coping with your life and everything it has experienced This exercise increases your body awareness.

Lie somewhere comfortable, preferably not on your bed (unless you are trying to get to sleep), and make sure you are warm enough. I like lying in the middle of the carpet with a cushion under my head and another under my knees. If you are feeling particularly bad, have a long bath or shower first or perhaps try the hot and cold water technique from level one before starting this.

Focus on your feet. Notice any feeling you can pick up from them. Become aware of everything you can feel, which foot feels more comfortable, whether you can feel your socks. Notice hot, cold, tingling, numbness, tightness, etc. Are there any areas you cannot feel? Does one foot feel bigger than the other? Is one sticking out to the side more than the other. Allow as much information to come through from your feet as possible. Then gently and slowly clench and relax your feet muscles.

While you are clenching it will be easier for you to feel exactly where your feet are. As you let go of them, see if you can stay in touch with how they feel. Does the felt sense of them disappear as you let go? As you relax, has the feeling changed? Can you feel tiredness, aching, tightness etc? If you can't feel anything, try clenching again. Just notice how they are.

Don't worry if the feelings are not clear to start off with. Ask yourself questions about the temperature, size, location, tightness, etc of each part and you may be able find answers them. For example, do both your feet feel the same height off the ground? You know they are physically at the same height, but sometimes one foot can feel much higher than the other, or much further away from your head than the other.

Then move on to the next set of muscles – the calves, and go through the same pattern of 1/ focusing on what you can feel in that place, 2/ clenching & relaxing, and 3/ feeling any reaction. This is not about making anything up, pretending or analysing. It is purely and simply about letting the feeling of your body come into your awareness. You don't have to do anything other than let this information come to you.

Carry on throughout your body. If you start getting involved with one part of the body then go into as much detail as you like. Don't be surprised if you start twitching or you suddenly feel changes of temperature or tingling or floaty sensations. Work all the way through your body focusing, clenching and relaxing and then noticing any reaction until you have worked through your neck, facial, and forehead muscles.

I recommend doing this at least 10 minutes or more everyday. At first you may not notice much. Don't worry. The more you do it, the more you will relax. The more you relax, the easier it is to feel.

If a major distraction keeps popping up, like a thought, a pain or ringing in the ears, that's normal, but just keep going back to the body. You may need to clench a few times before you can really focus on your body. Sometimes it takes a good ten minutes to really start being able to focus properly.

You can only ever really focus deeply on one thing at a time. If you are focusing on your foot with all your attention, then you won't be focusing on your tinnitus, or other aches and pains. Its fascinating how the more you *focus on parts of your body, the more you can influence how it feels. It gets more and more interesting the more experienced you get at it. For more information please read "Focusing" by Gendlin.*

This is about receiving information from the body. You are feeling not thinking. Noticing, not analysing. Just notice what its like being you....

If you find areas you can't feel at all, don't worry. Just become aware of the numb bits. How far does this numb, mystery area extend? Where can you start feeling clearly again around it?

These patterns change all the time, even while you are focusing on them. Your body will feel completely different in ten minutes time, on a different day, in a different mood.

Are there any emotional feelings held within? Is there sadness behind your tight chest, for example, or a feeling of anger behind your legs that feel like they want to kick? Perhaps there is a feeling of too much responsibility in your seized up neck and shoulders.

When your mind starts to wander, just simply refocus on your body and start noticing how you feel again. If you are a cerebral person (most tinnitus people are) use the clenching technique to really anchor your mind back into bodily sensation.

This is the perfect exercise for when you can't sleep. Tiredness is held in the body. If you come out of your thinking mind and connect with where the tiredness is held in the body, and how it feels, you are more likely to fall asleep.

Before you finish this exercise spend the last few minutes seeing if you can connect with what feels OK, comfortable, calm, safe, relaxed, easy, spacious etc. inside. What feels OK? Learning to get in touch with all these

> *positive feelings is one of the most positive things you can do. I wonder how good you are at doing this? Can you say what feels OK in you just now? I don't mean in your head, I mean something specific in your body that feels OK. There is usually plenty that feels OK, but we sometimes become experts at focusing on all the bad bits. Which do you do?*

I went through a stage of practising this for about 45 minutes every day. I was amazed at how the worst tantrums and feelings of despair and anxiety could eventually be settled just by maintaining my focus. If you persist with this technique you will become aware of all the energy and how it is stored in your body. This awareness helps you let go of things. I can do it these days to let go of a headache or bad mood. It takes practice, but with practice it works.

From my experience of treating literally hundreds of people with tinnitus, I have found that those who set up a programme of therapeutic support and spend time working through this technique, make good progress. Give yourself a few weeks trying this every day and see how it is for you. Most people generally get a lot out of it, especially if they have spent a whole lifetime living in their heads! Ring any bells?

Level 3: **Resigned**

At this level you start noticing that your tinnitus changes according to how you are. Get angry or frustrated, and it flares up. Do something that makes you happy or relaxed, then it seems to calm down. I have called this level RESIGNED because after all the stress and struggle of the two lower levels, something starts to give here and you start being able to accept your tinnitus. You start to realise that it is not the outside world that is directly responsible for this, but you have an important role too.

In the yellow level tinnitus behaves like one of those rather unsympathetic, old-school doctors that gives you stern advice. If you get upset, wound up, frantic or frightened the tinnitus will punish you. However, and this is the new revelation for this level that doesn't really exist at level two, if you really start looking after yourself, then the tinnitus does in fact back off. You are now coming to terms with the realisation that you can actually have an effect on it, after all. It may irritate you, and you may have to admit begrudgingly to yourself that maybe wallowing in misery and self-pity is not all that helpful. Here the first sense of taking responsibility starts creeping in as you start being a bit more constructive in thought, at least.

Now is the time to start listening to the advice your tinnitus is giving you. Of course you will notice if it gets worse. Rather than just focusing entirely on feeling distraught, at this stage you should start being able to step back a little and keep an eye on what is going on. The way out of tinnitus is to notice what makes you better. There will be times when you manage it better, or it backs off. When this happens look at what has been going on in your life, and pay attention to this. Your central nervous system is giving you invaluable information: it is telling you what is right for you, what works for you. Think of tinnitus as your in-built doctor who will give you better advice than anyone else. Pay attention to it, and you will find your way to well-being. This is the best ticket out of tinnitus.

Too much anger, frustration, tiredness, pressure, stress, living it up, stimulation, medicine, surgery, physical trauma, loud noise, exposure to cold, change, worry, alcohol, coffee, tea, sugar, unhealthy food, sex, intensity, racing in your head, all these can have an affect on tinnitus. The list is endless. I think the key phrase to be aware of is TOO MUCH.

More comfort, calm, support, manageability, predictable and safe routines, baths, healthy diet, gentle exercise, early nights, yoga, tai chi, meditation, letting go, down-time, fun, ease, snuggles, gardening etc makes your tinnitus back off.

For each person the specific triggers will be different, just as certain things will help certain people more than others. The more you work with your tinnitus and notice all the things that help it back off the better you will be. Some people think that nothing helps their tinnitus. If you are one of these, I gently suggest that you haven't paid enough attention to what helps. If you can reel off things that make it worse and cannot think of a single thing that helps, then this reveals a lot about your approach.

It can swing either way at this level. You can have a down day when tinnitus is giving you a stark reminder that you are not looking after yourself enough or that you have too much unprocessed baggage inside that needs therapy. You feel negative, but at least you manage to keep one eye open and notice what it was that set you off again, instead of drowning in it.

Other days you feel much better and admit that Julian's technique or that session with your therapist or the wonderful, happy long walk you had with a great friend has genuinely made you feel better. The tinnitus is still there but you feel better in yourself with it.

You are starting to ACCEPT that your relationship with tinnitus is a two-way process. It may feel like it has moved in but start working with your tinnitus and take its advice, and you will find your path to freedom.

As you start to realise your mind and body need attending to and looking after, you will start reaping the benefits. The moment you start finding things that work for you, then progress starts to accelerate. This gives you some relief, which means that you can let go more, focus on other things more, which in turn distracts you away from tinnitus, which in turn makes it easier to release.

Take positive action when tinnitus gets to you

One thing that really helps at this stage is to get into a habit of doing something positive every time you find yourself reacting negatively to tinnitus. Literally every time your mind starts fretting, take a few deep breaths (see breathing technique at the end of level 6), go for a walk, lie on the floor and do the clenching and relaxing exercise, or anything that makes you feel better. If you get into a regular habit of meeting your negative experience with a positive one, you will start to associate tinnitus with something good.

In your subconscious every time tinnitus starts threatening, your body will get used to starting to relax and feel better. It doesn't matter if it is a hot shower, yoga or having a sing or rubbing your feet, just get into a regular habit of meeting tinnitus with something positive, and it will very quickly start to matter less. The last thing you should do is stew in negativity! This compounds the whole pattern. Take positive action instead.

I used to just take my focus to whatever felt good in my body. I asked the question: can I find something that feels OK just now? I would take a moment and find something warm, comfortable, strong, clear, free, loose, calm, smooth, centred and then focus on it. Sounds simple, doesn't it, but it is amazing how few people with tinnitus know what feels okay inside. Its there all the time, its just that we tend not to connect with it.

Buy yourself a foot-spa, create a space in your living room where you can practise relaxing every time you need to. Leave the cushions and blankets out because you may well need to do your relaxation techniques more than once on some days. It's useful to aim to bring in something positive every time your tinnitus triggers a negative response in you. You may think you stew and think about your tinnitus all the time. Well, in actual fact, you may surprise yourself how much less you focus on it than you think. I challenge you to sit for five minutes and focus on your tinnitus. I can almost guarantee that your mind will wander onto something else!

If you are reading this and you haven't yet started the process of bringing in support and looking after yourself better, then at some stage you may need to look at why this isn't happening. Check in with that saboteur in you, the part that says, "This won't work. It'll never go," and so on. Be honest and ask yourself what is holding you back. If you stay stuck at any level, there will be an important reason for doing so. What is stopping you from getting therapy, practising the techniques? Are you one of these people that has to cope by themselves? Is it hard letting support in? Does it feel like a failure or too self-indulgent attending to your own needs? Be really honest, I dare you. Deep down inside you'll know.

Believe it or not, I have met some people who crave everyone's sympathy with tinnitus, as if they have never had enough attention in their lives. Getting better removes the attention they are getting. So, as a result, they end up doing everything in their power to keep their tinnitus in place. Others don't want to get better because they can't be bothered, or actually quite like being miserable. Sounds unbelievable, but its true. I regularly experience people who, the moment they start getting better and start understanding what tinnitus is all about, discontinue treatment. It seems that there is too much to lose by getting better. We must never underestimate the power of symptoms and how they can give us what we need!

The fact that you are reading this suggests that you want to get better.

So with Doctor Tinnitus checking up on you, the challenge here is to listen to the health advice it is giving you and learn from it rather than fight it. You should be starting to realise that anything that creates resistence or a struggle is not helpful for tinnitus.

Let tinnitus show you what works for you and what makes you better. You will have your own unique things that work for you as an individual. To be frank, your tinnitus will make sure you learn what these are. It will reward you when you do the right thing, and punish you when you lose your rag, or overdo things. I have shared some of the things that helped my own tinnitus, and what made it worse. You will find what works for you. That's what tinnitus is for. Finding your health. Now there's a thought!

This next technique is absolutely essential. Please do it today. Work on it over the next few weeks. You may be surprised how revealing it is about you.

Technique 3: Better and worst list

Get a piece of paper and put a plus sign and a minus sign at the top. List all the things that you notice make you feel better under the plus. Whenever you find you are having a good day, take a look at what is going on add it to the list. Do the same with the negative side and know what things activate your tinnitus and make it worse.

Stick this list on a prominent place like the fridge for a month or two and build up more awareness of what works for you. Obviously you may reach some important conclusions about you, your lifestyle and your activities by the end of this. It may help you to become clear about what to avoid and what to work on.

You may feel that your tinnitus is fairly constant. If this is the case, notice when you feel things are more manageable, or when things become more unbearable. People often think their tinnitus is fixed, but on closer inspection notice it actually changes much more than they realised. What we believe is the case is very often different to the way things really are.

Level 4: **Motivated**

Notice there is a thick line across the matrix between levels three and four.

This is an enormous transition zone that I have noticed in tinnitus people. Once you can get to level four, then it's pretty much downhill all the way. Whereas the first three levels have been unpleasant and challenging, once you cross the threshold into green, then suddenly you start to discover that tinnitus is no longer the nasty, bossy old tyrant that it was, robbing you of peace and sanity. To the contrary, this condition seems to have turned into quite a useful healthometer showing you what's right for you and what's not.

Sounds pretty like level three, but the crucial difference here is motivation. Now that you have taken responsibility for your own tinnitus, and accept that it is there and you yourself have a massive impact on it, you are starting to get a sense of what is needed for you to be well. After the uphill struggle of the lower levels, in level four you are MOTIVATED enough to keep on going all by yourself. You have experienced how tinnitus can back off and you enjoy taking good care of yourself because it feels so much better to do so. It is worth it for the relief alone.

At this level there is a sense of much more space. Tinnitus is still in the house, but has moved out of your room into its own. It's still there but it doesn't bug you so much. At last there is a sense of it being manageable and you can get on with things.

Of course there are still bad days where it flares up, but you are starting to develop that all-important sense of knowing from direct experience that it will back off again the moment you go to bed early, or have a break or do whatever it is do you to feel good and relax. Tinnitus is not a threat anymore. Now you can stare it in the face and have a healthy respect for it. You are not controlled by it now, but you listen carefully to what this symptom is trying to teach you.

You are here most likely because you have started benefiting from a few months of therapeutic support. You have directly experienced that it is possible to feel much better than you were used to and are possibly starting to get in touch with more important underlying issues that fuel the tinnitus pattern in the first place. In short at this level you have developed a real sense of how to be well from time to time.

You have become INDEPENDENT and don't need to be badgered into taking more care of yourself. You already have a good sense of what works for you and how good it makes you feel, and you are starting to reap the benefits. You've got out of the hole and it feels such a relief. Tinnitus has turned into a pretty good TEACHER and you are rapidly finding out what is right for you.

Level four on the matrix is the time when you start considering what really matters to you, and what changes you need to make in your life so that it can become more wonderful. It's decision time. As you become much more caring towards yourself and start treating yourself with kindness and consideration, you start to get a sense of what you really want. Certainly the things you don't want become loud and clear and easier to weed out.

I suddenly realised one day how tough I had been on myself, and how I had to do do do, achieve, be the best, prove my point, and try and try again. It slowly dawned on me that this was one of the most important underlying causes of tinnitus in me, this inability to just accept things just as they are and let myself be good enough as I am right now. Talking to hundreds of tinnitus people, I started to see how we all seem to be driven, and unable to appreciate that we are probably good enough already. Many of us seem to feel guilty about doing nothing. We simply give ourselves a hard time.

It was at this stage of level four that I started to treat myself with more kindness, and this made a huge difference. I started to let go of a need to be perfect and successful, and started to allow myself to be just good enough. It really was such a relief.

The technique at the end of this section helps develop this sense of loving kindness towards oneself. It is extraordinarily simple and yet if you do it properly, can turn out to be a memorable and powerful experience.

When I was passing through this stage there was quite a delayed effect on improvement. If I got a bad cold, lost my temper or went through a stressful patch, my tinnitus would rear up and start treating me like a grouchy doctor or sergeant major again. At lower levels I would have panicked at this wobble and would have needed to get support from my craniosacral therapist. However at level 4, having built up some experience of knowing what helps me and how to manage my tinnitus, I would just get back on the support wagon and do my relaxation exercises, especially the clench and relax technique at the end of level 3. I would do this for perhaps an hour at a time and feel immediately more centred and in control. However it might take me a week or so to settle back to the improved level of symptoms that I was experiencing before the wobble.

In retrospect I think I did quite well considering that the only regular support I allowed into my life was bi-weekly craniosacral therapy. Today I find my ability to cope with wobbles is better than ever, because I have a firmly established and regularly visited support network: psychotherapist, craniosacral therapist, a week off every month, a good diet, a strengthening Buddhist foundation, friends, daily swimming, and a wonderful partner.

I am aware that this may sound intimidating for some, and may get your Saboteur thinking, "But I can't do all that, it's too expensive, takes up too much time, I don't believe in anything, etc." Believe me, I used to be just as hard on myself and have no help at all like perhaps many of you who are reading this now. Tinnitus loves lurking in the lives of people who drive themselves to the limit and who are hard on themselves.

However the more I started giving myself time and space to be supported, the more I felt the deep benefits of it creep into all areas of my life. We are not meant to be alone and cope with masses of stress unaided. People who tend to do this (like me, for example) have often needed to cope and pull themselves together right from day one, as a result of the way they were brought into the world and brought up. Early patterns established by our mothering and family dynamic are powerful forces that turn us into the driven achievers and restless souls that tinnitus lives through. And yet, thanks to tinnitus, I discovered this fairly early on, and found that life is much happier and more manageable with plenty of resources to draw on.

As you get stronger and look after yourself more, when life rocks the boat as it surely will, it gradually takes less and less to reactivate your tinnitus. These days it takes one hell of a cold, or a massive amount of fear, anger, stress, coffee, alcohol to bring it back. I'm generally free of it, but if a tiny whistle flickers on the horizon, it is usually gone by the morning.

The point I want to share with you is that the more you look after yourself, the stronger your whole nervous system becomes. Your immunity and ability to manage things slowly gets better and better. The delay between tinnitus flaring up and the amount of time needed to get back on track does get shorter and shorter depending on how readily you are prepared to look after yourself.

Even with powerful illnesses or enormous challenges like bereavement, the more we open up to support, help and nourishment from others, the better we will cope. You all know this. What I am saying is no great revelation. The fact that you have tinnitus is not because you don't know the effects of a healthy diet, good friendship, or the benefits of therapy. It is possibly because you do not allow yourself enough of these things! You may be depriving yourself of all the things you long for and need because you have probably had to be tough, grit your teeth, and cope without them in the past. This is learnt behaviour that seems "normal."

Why not rest, enjoy yourself a bit more, let go of the need to be brilliant, successful, wealthy, perfect, admirable, etc, and start just being OK? This is a really interesting question.

To show the consequences of this, 10 years ago a cup of coffee made me spin and feel nauseous, and my tinnitus flared up. Now I have one every day and thrive on it with no effect on symptoms. The same is true for wine, or staying up late. I had to be ultra careful of what I exposed myself to, or what I ate, but these days I am slackening the reins a lot and am getting away with it. This is possible because I have allowed myself to let go, switch off and recharge. I have plenty of time off, and instead of lots of money, I have lots of free time. In fact downtime has become sacred for me. I'm not encouraging bad habits here, but I am saying that, with tinnitus, when you really start looking after yourself, your constitution gradually gets better and better. Bear in mind that it's not just tinnitus that improves. You may well experience:

- Better digestion
- Improved memory
- Stronger nerves
- Clearer thinking
- Better sleep
- More stable emotions
- More energy
- Stronger immunity
- A longer life
- A happier general mood

You are not just letting go of tinnitus, you are bringing yourself out of a body stress response which will have an effect on all these factors. Your tinnitus is your in-built personalised friend that will show you what is right for you. If you let it work for you, you will find much greater health benefits. Let your tinnitus guide you in a healthy direction that is tailor-made and perfect just for you. The more you do the right thing, the more it will back off.

The challenge at this level is to develop confidence and know that you will be OK every time you get knocked down a level by something challenging that comes along. When you get rattled by whatever trigger that comes along, setting off your alarm bells again, here you will learn from experience that it will go anyway, as long as you adopt your coping strategies that will be becoming clear at this level.

What is the situation touching inside you that you need to deal with? Take this to therapy and explore it. You cannot change the outside world but you certainly can change the way you deal with it inside. If someone makes you angry, there is something important inside of you that is reacting to it. It's not just them, its you too.

Confidence in the fact that things will be alright each time your tinnitus flares up increases every time you manage to survive and recover from one of these episodes. The more this happens, the stronger you will get. You may get worse when you are overtired, but you know that a few early nights will make it better. An infuriating

> ### *Technique 4: Knowing what matters to you*
> *One day I sat down and made a long list of all the things that I loved. I started slowly but after a few minutes I really got into it. Much to my surprise I ended up spending a couple of hours doing this and amazingly it brought up tears, and a much greater sense of clarity. I really recommend this.*
>
> *Tell everyone to leave you alone for a while. No phone calls or interruptions are allowed. Get a large piece of paper and evenly spaced out all over it, write different categories of things that you could describe from your life, eg: people, animals, places, work, dreams, memories, plants, smells, activities, hobbies, body sensations, thoughts, pieces of music, philosophies, writers, poets, and so on. Then in clusters around these words list all the different things that you love and that really matter to you. Give yourself plenty of time.*
>
> *If this sounds too complicated, just start writing a list of all the things you love. Make it as long as possible. Keep adding to it.*
>
> *It sounds so simple, but as you do it you learn something important about yourself. Sometimes you can feel something open up inside. It can leave you feeling warm, expansive and quite simply joyful. NB Beware of the saboteur, as it really likes sabotaging this one! Thoughts like: what a load of nonsense, what on earth is this going to achieve, that's too new-age for me, etc can actually be just a way of avoiding your heart. I made a decision to change my career path after doing this. It helped me get a sense of the kind of work I needed to do.*

situation may set your head ringing, but if you spend an hour focussing on body sensation then you know you will feel better. This knowledge becomes more and more unshakable, and the gathering confidence takes root and strengthens like a tree.

As you really start getting better on a deeper level, you can be incredibly empowering for other people who are suffering with tinnitus. Your wellness and recovery from symptoms is inspiring and motivating and gives them hope and direction.

At this stage you start to get a sense of your body being the place where all your life experience is held, RIGHT NOW. With all the body work you have been receiving, you know that this is the place where blocked issues and undigested life experience can slowly be released and freed up. Working on the body directly helps the mind, and vice versa. They are inseparable. You have stopped treating yourself like a workhorse at this stage. It becomes harder to feed yourself rubbish and flog yourself to exhaustion. Your tinnitus is teaching you this.

Technique 5: How do you view yourself?

Try doing the same thing, but this time base it on yourself. Write category words that could relate to you like: personality, looks, talents, strengths, interests, loves, originalities, clothes, taste, intelligence, desires, contributions, relationships etc. and then list all the good qualities about you. This can be an incredibly revealing exercise. You may well end up staring at the truth of how you treat yourself, view yourself and drive yourself around like a donkey. This can be a real heart-melter. Once again, tell the saboteur to jump in a lake while you have a deeper look at yourself. If you do this properly, you can really start to bring in a whole new depth to looking after yourself, a bit like becoming your own therapist. It literally helps you warm to yourself and appreciate you in a way that you quite often miss!

If there is any resistance to doing this, look at it. What are you afraid of? What is stopping you from loving and appreciating yourself?

Technique 6: Running commentary

This is the technique that I use most often, probably three times a week for at least half and hour at a time. It is excellent for slowing down a busy head and for developing the ability to witness what is going on in your body at any one time. I am not joking or exaggerating when I say this has changed my life.

Create some time and space where you will not be disturbed for twenty minutes or so. Get yourself into a comfortable position and settle yourself into body awareness mode. By this level you should be quite good at doing this. If you are still struggling try some of the other techniques mentioned in the lower levels to settle your awareness into your body. If you mind is really racing, then have a shower or a bath first. Massage your feet and take some deep slow breaths.

I prefer doing this lying down on the floor with a big cushion supporting my knees and just the right number of pillows to take the pressure off my neck. It always feels comforting for me to lie under a blanket. Get into a comfortable position for you.

When you are ready, start giving a running commentary out loud of what is going on in your body, describing what you can feel. It may seem ridiculous at first to talk out loud by yourself, but speaking is in itself very focussing. Anything that helps you focus will help you settle.

So it might sound like this. "I'm lying here and feeling a bit hunched up around my upper back, and I don't feel evenly placed on the floor. In fact my hips feel tilted to the right and my chest seems to be pointing to the left, and my head is tight." You suddenly sigh deeply. "I've just taken a deep breath and I feel a bit more relaxed."

As you lie there just describe any sensations that come up into your awareness. One moment it might be an itch here and then a twitch there. Suddenly you might become aware of a pain in your jaw or a tightness at the base of your back. Just notice all the physical sensations of how hot or cold you are, what feels light or heavy, free or tight, tingly, jangly or smooth.

The secret here is not to go looking for stuff. Much more interesting is to let the information come to you. You're lying back and at any moment some sensation may come into your awareness. You have no idea what the next thing will be or where it will come from. It's a bit like going to the cinema, you relax and let the information come. When it appears just describe it and then wait for the next thing to arise.

From time to time you may start thinking about something. This is quite normal. Don't worry about it. When this happens its really useful to say, "I'm thinking again," and just wait for the next felt sense to appear. If you find yourself thinking about something a lot, maybe take a deep breath and just settle your awareness back into the world of hot/cold, long/short, big/small, agitated/calm, floaty/solid.

I particularly like feeling how far my head is from my feet. Sometimes this feels a long way away, other times it feels short. Comparing the length of your legs is often an easy way to get back in touch with the body. Even though they are the same length, they may feel very different in length, height off the ground, size, weight etc. It can be surprising how things feel.

When pain comes up just notice what it is like. Is there a sense of pressure or does it feel like something wants to move? Is there numbness around the area or is it tingly? See if you can feel exactly where the pain is located, or notice if it is out of focus and slightly dispersed. Describe it out aloud. If tinnitus comes up, just say, "I'm focusing on my tinnitus," and wait for the next felt thing to appear.

The mind gets bored quite easily and will not stay with the tinnitus before long, as it will be distracted by something else. This can be quite revealing. If you try and focus on the tinnitus, after a few seconds you will find you are thinking about something else. If you don't believe me, try timing yourself! I bet you cannot focus on your tinnitus for more than one minute without your mind wandering onto something else. We all think we spend the whole time thinking about it, but the reality is very different. This might be quite surprising. It was for me, and actually very liberating. Anyway, where was I? If your mind starts wandering just go back to the body and wait for the next sensation to appear.

When you dry up and feel like you have run out of things to describe, this is really interesting. Just wait. Soon something else will pop up.

Learning to live in this state of body awareness is incredibly helpful. It's like discovering an alternative to the normal thinking process. It takes you beneath all the mental chatter and puts you in touch with how you feel. You actually develop a much more accurate sense of how you are. We all know how our minds can run away with themselves and lead us into worry, exaggeration, fear and irrational thoughts.

When you get proficient at this, you can chose to focus inside in the middle of an argument or when you are fearful. This changes the dynamic totally and gives you a lot more options. Watch and enjoy how your mind really slows down!

Level 5: Letting go

Your relationship with tinnitus really moves on at this level as this is the stage where it starts losing its grip on your awareness. Now you are entering the phase where you can start letting go of your need to monitor it all the time. You begin to regard it as a helpful indicator of how you are feeling, rather than a problem to be solved. What distinguishes this level from previous ones is that your awareness is no longer locked within your inner world. Here you are taking a larger perspective on things. You are able to sit back and witness how your body and mind affect each other, without getting swamped by feelings, reactions or symptoms. There is more space in your awareness. Letting go is the level where there is enough room for you to have an objective look at how tinnitus is intertwined with your life. You are realising that the way you are inside affects the way the world and life seem on the outside. You are becoming able to witness yourself from the outside and know what you are like, rather than just being locked way, unaware, inside your patterns.

This larger perspective and more spacious approach helps you let go. For example, rather than get angry and sit in a stew of boiling reactions, you notice how a situation is affecting you and you are able to work through your own reactions rather than just fling something back at the other person. If something irritates you then you are able to stay in touch with your reaction and process that rather than retaliate.

You recognise that tinnitus will come and go depending on how you are, and this no longer takes up much attention. It has become so NORMALISED that you no longer react emotionally to its comings and goings, and you no longer find it interesting or such an issue anymore.

Up to now tinnitus has had quite a lot of influence over you and your daily life, but here we are entering the stage where you genuinely start having a lot more choice. You can focus on it from time to time, but it is not important. At this level you can may well become bored of it, to be frank, and you start forgetting about it and focussing on other things.

If someone asks you how it is, you have to stop and find it first, before you can answer. It is there but, there is a sense that it is really backing off and getting quieter. Tinnitus has moved out and become a next door neighbour that can be noisy from time to time.

Taking more responsibility for how well you feel, you are now much more on top of how your nervous system reacts.

When a challenging situation comes up that could tip you over into great fury, frustration, despair, tiredness or any of the states of mind that give rise to tinnitus, you now have the ability to chose how you will react.

You can either lose your rag, wobble, get distraught and start fighting against tinnitus all over again, and find yourself spiralling down a level or two. Alternatively you can process it in your own way, or take it to your therapist/bodyworker and get support in releasing your reactions.

At this level you know how to take things off the simmer and switch off. You have learnt to process things in a manageable way, and spend much more time relaxing and looking after your reactions to life.

Taking care of yourself has become second nature. You know your limits and no longer take on too many commitments. You know when you need to put some time aside to get yourself back on track. When you have a set back, increasing confidence in how to manage yourself keeps you calm and motivates you to go in the right direction. In a crisis you know that in a day or two you will feel better again.

Tinnitus has taught you the cost of having a tantrum or stewing in negative thought processes. Because you have become much kinder to yourself, you can stop yourself from flying into a state of overwhelm.

I remember when my tinnitus was bad I was stuck in victim mode a lot of the time. If something terrible happened, I would feel that the world was unfair and I was the unfortunate mug at the end of the line. I would implode and then get really frustrated with myself, sulk, brood and then, as if that wasn't enough, I would dislike myself for being weak, and not good enough. What a nightmare that was!

These days if something terrible happens, I notice where it affects me in the body. I really get in touch with these feelings and let them take their course over a few hours or days. I notice how my mind reacts, consider what I need, and then set about getting these needs met. That might mean asking for a hug, getting support, or just processing my reactions with a therapist. This approach is so much more manageable and I bounce back readily, rather than exacerbating the problem with spiralling negative reactions. I treat myself well, instead of like a tyrant.

When we can witness our experience instead of being locked up inside it, this creates far more possibilities. Its the difference between, "I am bloody furious," and "Gosh, that's interesting, there is some anger there, and I can really feel my jaw clenching, or a feeling like I want to run away." The first is lost in the emotion of it and can feel pretty overwhelming, whereas the second is much more manageable, has more space and is in touch with the body's reaction. Getting in touch with the body's reaction means we can directly meet something we can let go of.

We all have the power to manage ourselves really well. Learning how to do this is one of the huge benefits of therapy work. We learn life skills that make everything more manageable.

We can let go into life more, no longer needing to cling on to our fears so much. I think everything boils down to love or fear. A lot of working through tinnitus is about letting go of fear and embracing a more loving approach to ourselves and the life around us. Just knowing we have support there and that we can rely on a class of tai chi, meditation, chi gung, yoga, is deeply comforting. The extra energy and clarity we get from being more centred and together makes everything more manageable.

At this stage you can sit quietly in a room and become aware of tinnitus and be OK with it. It has become a familiar part of you and that feels fine. Just like being able to sit down, focus on a shoe and become aware of how that feels, at this level you can chose to do the same with the ringing in your ears. There may be a sense of it there if you really try and focus on it, but you do not need to do this anymore. Of course you can feel your shoe all the time its on your foot, but you are not focussing on it, so it is not there in your awareness. Tinnitus can become as important as feeling your shoe!

This is such a useful place to get to with tinnitus because it is here that your perception of it changes and it goes quiet or disappears. You realise that if you are not thinking about it, it is not there. You catch yourself in silence and then looking for it, you recreate it again. You start to experience how fragile, tentative and unimportant the whole symptom is. It really has lost any power over you.

The challenge at this level is to stay friends with tinnitus when something negative brings it back. Do you need to check if it is still there? This is where we need to work on

Technique 7: Audiovisualisation Technique

People with tinnitus are often given a masker to generate noise in their ears, which distracts them from their tinnitus. As they focus less and less on it, they become much more likely to let go of symptoms. Here I am offering a technique that can help you create an alternative to a masker using one of the most powerful tools you have – your imagination.

It's easy to close our eyes and picture the face of someone we love, or remember a beautiful beach or view across the mountains. We can also remember sounds easily, and this technique develops this skill into an interesting tool for managing tinnitus.

If you practice this audiovisualisation a few times, you will find that your ability to focus on imagined sound will get clearer and clearer. The more your mind becomes focussed, the more choice you have with what you experience. With practice you can learn to hear a waterfall all around you while you are travelling on the Underground! More importantly, you can learn to hear a pleasant sound in your imagination that is much more agreeable than just sitting there with tinnitus, if its still around.

letting go of the need to monitor it. You know it is just a healthy warning, showing you that you need to look after yourself again. It is trying to help you. Appreciate it when it pops up into your awareness and thank it for reminding you to look after yourself a bit more.

What is happening inside you when it appears? This is the most useful enquiry: look into your reaction to the tinnitus rather than the tinnitus itself. What is it telling you about yourself? Are you a perfectionist, full of frustration, pushing yourself too hard? What is the emotional state that is driving this reaction?

> *You will need 20 minutes of uninterrupted time to yourself for this exercise. Sit comfortably somewhere reasonably quiet where you won't be disturbed. Read this slowly, and as you go along really allow your imagination to ignite and become vivid and colourful.*
>
> *Get comfortable and take a couple of deep breaths. Clench and relax each part of your body working from your feet up to your face to help your mind settle and become more focused.*
>
> *Imagine you are standing next to a small waterfall in a forest. Notice what it looks like. What colour is it? Is it in the shade or is the sun shining on it? Walk up closer to it and feel the cool dampness against your face and smell the earthy moss filling the air.*
>
> *Hear how the water is trickling down between the rocks. Stop for a moment and really listen to this in your imagination. In places you can hear it dripping. Hear each drip dropping down into a pool of water. In other places you can hear it gushing more constantly and spattering against the*

rocks. You may need to close your eyes for a few seconds to really allow this to form in your mind.

Get closer and hear it through your left ear. Imagine the sound coming in through your left hand side as if the waterfall was pouring down just to the left of the chair where you are sitting. Then, slowly imagine you can move the waterfall behind you and hearing it behind your neck and back. You could almost shiver at the thought of cold water running down your back. Then slowly continue to move the waterfall so you can hear it to the right of your chair. Take your time with this and enjoy all the qualities of running water and how it sounds around you. Close your eyes and give this a try just now. Is it easier to imagine the sound on one side more than the other?

In another part of the fall you notice the water is gushing at quite a rate. Notice how it is spattering noisily onto a large rock at the bottom. The noise is uneven and sometimes quickens with a rush of more water, and sometimes slows down and sounds quieter.

Bring the waterfall round to the front of you. Get ready to turn it into a raging torrent. Notice that it has started to rain. You can hear it falling in the forest all around, pattering on the ground. Suddenly there is a clap of thunder and the sky darkens. The rain steadily gets heavier and heavier until it is spattering against the leaves of the trees, and pounding the ground everywhere. Let it turn into a tropical downpour of heavy, fat raindrops, lashing the trees and the splashing into puddles all around. Can you still hear the waterfall? The noise is so loud now that if you needed to talk to someone you would have to shout.

The water is now tumbling and crashing down the fall. Hear that deep pounding sound as the wall of water plunges into the pool sending a foaming mass of bubbling water and spray in all directions. Feel the cool spray flying in your face and enjoy the invigorating feeling. Another clap of thunder and now the rain is lashing every square inch of forest. You can't

> *see more than ten yards ahead through the thick spray everywhere. The falls are crashing down in front. It is so loud that you can feel your chest booming with the pounding of the water against the rocks.*
>
> *Slowly allow the darkness to lift, and the sky brightens and slowly the rain starts to calm down. The falls are still raging but the sound of the rain has gone. A ray of sunshine comes through and you are left with just the sound of water cascading into deep pools. Gradually let the water level subside and die back to a trickle. You start noticing drops dripping off the rocks and sploshing into the pools. You can hear drops falling off trees into puddles. You start to hear birds singing in the branches. Let the sound go back to a gentle and relaxing background noise.*

As you read this, I bet you heard lots of noise in your mind. Its almost impossible not to. Try this again but with your eyes closed and you are in charge this time. Really enjoy your own creation of sound and get into as much detail as possible.

What is extraordinary with this exercise is that if you get into it, your mind lets go of tinnitus completely and really focuses on what you want it to. With practice you can really streamline your ability to hear in a sharp focused way which can help clarify silence away from tinnitus. I have found my ability to hear silence has been helped with this practice.

Once you have practiced this a couple of times, you can now try it when the TV is on, or when music is playing or while you are travelling on the train. In your imagination you can learn to focus all your attention on this imagined sound, even if there is a lot of noise and distraction around you. The more you enjoy and explore this technique, the more you will be able to stay focused. I often imagine the sound of a waterfall crashing around me if I have to take public transport. It makes me feel well.

I enjoy imagining the feeling of standing in the waterfall, so I can hear, smell, taste and feel the cool water rushing down all around me. I have got so used to doing this that it actually becomes invigorating, calming and refreshing. It is the perfect antidote to unpleasant situations that could potentially stress me.

The best sounds to imagine are ones that you love, whether it is the sound of your mother singing, the wind in the trees, children playing outside, or your best friend laughing. Whichever sound you choose, play with it in your mind. The more you change it and explore the possibilities, the deeper you can go into this part of your mind.

Here are some more interesting audiovisualisations to try out:

Song

Find a recording of a song you know really well and love. Sit down and play it from beginning to end and remind yourself of the words. Then when it has finished, sit in silence and play it again in your mind's ear. See how far you can get. Can you hear all the words right up to the end?

When a new verse starts, change the voice to that of another singer. Try turning it into Welsh men's choir, or that of an opera diva. Try to hear your own voice. Maybe you decide to hear an instrumental version with strings only and no voice at all. Have fun. The more ridiculous and funny it is, the more you are likely to find it easy to focus on.

Have the singer move up close and sing into your left ear, then into the other one. Have them change position and walk around you. Chose someone gorgeous and enjoy the coquettish way they are singing to you. The sexier the voice the easier it is to focus on.

Then imagine you are the conductor who wants to put them through their paces and speed up the tempo. Hear them struggling to keep up, then slow it right down.

> **Laughter**
> Hear yourself laughing, then hear people in your family starting to laugh too. Then hear people outside laughing, until the whole world is laughing loudly. Sitting on the bus, plane or tube, imagine how each person would laugh. Notice how each person laughs so differently. Waiting at the check-out watch people and imagine what each person would sound like howling with laughter. This is really good fun and puts you into a good mood even on an underground train in rush hour.

With a bit of practice, all these enjoyable sounds can take your mind off tinnitus. It is quite hard to hear your tinnitus when you are really focused on sounds in your mind. They lift your spirits and have a powerful impact on your mood and how relaxed you feel. I really encourage you to have a go, use your imagination and discover how much you can influence your whole central nervous system for the better!

Level 6: **Empowered**

Well tinnitus has moved out now and lives in the neighbourhood. But you've become friends, and you know that if you get out of kilter with your body it will be there to help you find your centre again and re-establish a good sense of health. Most of the time you are not aware of tinnitus, but if you sit in silence you could probably find it again. Equally, you might just notice silence.

The crucial point here is that you have practically no interest in checking up on tinnitus anymore. Why should you bother? There's no problem. You know that if you look for it, you might find it there just sounding in the far distance sometimes, but there is no need to check this out. Your tinnitus is no longer important, so you don't check up on it.

If you are operating at this level, you have probably already established an excellent support network, have plenty of downtime and really know how to look after yourself. Your lifestyle is balanced, in as far as you match the amount of energy you give out through work with plenty of nourishing time for yourself to relax and appreciate all the good things in life. There is an equal amount of give and take. Your central nervous system can rest in a state of neutral so that it can either burn off energy in activity, or switch off and recharge again when resting.

Having given yourself plenty of time to let go, process and relax, your system is able to function "normally" again. Just like a battery, our nervous systems do need to recharge for us to feel well.

The well-being you have at this level is there because you have learnt to let help in, and get support when you need it. You have got into the habit of taking any difficulty or discomfort to a body worker or therapist whenever you feel overwhelmed, and probably air your issues regularly with good friends. Nothing builds up too much for you to handle. When big challenges come along you have some sense of how best to cope with them and know where to go for help. This in itself is deeply comforting and reassuring. In short, you can relax in a position of strength and are ready for action if need be.

Tinnitus has turned into an incredibly useful guide leading you to a much greater sense of health and well-being. Helping you get in touch with yourself at a much deeper level opens up a whole new way of being and a new approach to your sense of self.

All the body work helps you get in touch with your body's felt sense at a deep level, and you start to become aware of energetic reactions. You can focus on internal feelings in a much more detailed way and feel changes in temperature, tingling, floatiness, a sense of expansion, and an opening up into a more sensitive connection to the space around you.

I have found Craniosacral therapy and Core Process Psychotherapy to be particularly good for developing a greater sensitivity of internal awareness. The gentle hand contacts of cranial work often remain still in the same place for long periods of time. This means you are not distracted by lots of external stimulation and your focus naturally goes inside and you become aware of internal changes as you lie there. Equally a Core Process Psychotherapist can help guide you into bodily experience so that as you are working through each issue, he or she can help you get in touch with how it is affecting the body and how you feel inside. There is always a certain part of our body that is reacting to each situation. Getting in touch with this can really help transform how we hold on to things.

At first it seems like magic, but then you slowly start to realise that the body knows what it needs to do. All you do is just get out of the way and let go into the support. It is like an inbuilt intelligence and organising force gathers momentum, and starts helping things realign effortlessly. It can be deeply inspiring to feel something naturally sorting itself out inside you, without any apparent effort. There is most definitely a force that knows what it wants inside. Learning how to let go deeply allows this life force or dynamic organising system to come more and more into affect. The more I have learnt to let go into this centering and organising force, the more I have been able to release aches and pains in my body and become less dependent on medicines and manipulations to sort myself out. This arising energy or life force is available to all of us all the time. We just need to unblock our connection to it arising at every instant in our core.

These days, when I have a pain in my body, I lie down and settle into a deep state of calm. This involves getting in touch with all the things that feel fine, calm and comfortable in your body. Once I have a strong sense of this, I then go into the pain and really get a sense of how it feels inside. If it is bad pain I will only take my focus to the edge of it, without dropping right into it, to keep things manageable.

Approaching the pain, sometimes you feel like something wants to move inside it, or like a pressure wants to release. I spend time getting in touch with the buzzing, throbbing or tightness that is there. After about ten minutes or so just focussing really carefully on it and connecting with it, I start to link the area of pain up to the rest of the body. So if my heart is hurting and feeling tight, I notice how it connects to each shoulder, how my breathing affects it, whether it feels tight towards the front or the back of my body. I literally feel all around it and explore this felt-sense. Sometimes I can feel something changing. When you widen your field of awareness out to include the whole body, the pain can actually start freeing up before your eyes. It is extraordinary what we can do just by focussing. This is well known amongst people who meditate a lot, and is an ability that develops with practice.

We are lucky having so much available to help our health with all the technical advances in health and medicine. However body-awareness is a huge underrated resource that we can tap into, transforming how we feel. To be really healthy we need to combine external scientific approaches with internal process and awareness. Both are good, and having both working together is best.

I believe we need an integrated approach to health where both an internal awareness is combined with external science and expertise. Ken Wilber's approach to an integral way of life explains this clearly and simply in his book, "A Theory of Everything." It makes sense.

Wisdom relating to health has been around for thousands of years and has always worked for those who bother to enquire into it. The problem is that it needs you to start the enquiry. I am not against drugs or surgery, but tinnitus is a symptom that responds directly to our internal process and how we treat ourselves. Rather than resort to drugs or surgery which can be extremely helpful in certain situations, I personally to try and sort things out inside first, and enter a very real possibility of getting better, before resorting to more invasive treatment.

Bodywork and therapy opens up this inner world and is of immense value. Stay with it long enough and you will develop an insight into the energetic realm, if you don't have it already. This can completely change the way you approach yourself and the world around you. It quite literally opens up a completely different way of being.

The first session of craniosacral therapy was a direct experience of my body not as just flesh and bones, but a container of different kinds of energy resonating in a fascinating and powerful way. Like many people I am sensitive enough to feel this energetic perspective loud and clear and therapy has increased my awareness of the body as a container of moving fluids and energies. This has a big impact on your health, mind and your body.

Understanding how we develop psychologically is of immense help as well. When we start to become aware of our patterns of behaviour and where they come from, this too can really help us develop strength which helps us slowly, slowly, over a period of time, start to let go of our normal way of acting in the world.

Taking a deeper look at the typical tinnitus person for example. As a child he/she was not given enough love early on. As a result he/she grows into a highly driven and competitive person trying to prove to themselves and the remote parent that they are worthy enough of receiving love and attention. They spend their whole lives trying to fill this sense of emptiness inside and create the ideal conditions for symptoms like tinnitus to appear. Every day of their life is filled with a prevailing sense of never having enough, never being satisfied or at peace. In this book I have mentioned many surface causes for tinnitus such as: getting divorced, working too hard, exhaustion.

However if we look into the deeper causes, what really matters underneath is that there is very often a lack of loving continuity, guaranteed on-going protection and safety provided by our parents. Our earliest experience sets up the strongest reactions that form the central structure of our personalities. A less than ideal beginning can set up patterns of neediness and frustration that in later life lead to tinnitus. This is where psychotherapy can be immensely beneficial.

Slowly we can uncover the deep cause for our inner struggle that lies at the core of our being. When we can come to terms with our deepest struggles then something literally comes to terms, that is, something stops, and settles. As tinnitus is something that thrives on internal resistance, if we are able to accept and find peace with our innermost experience, then tinnitus doesn't stand a chance!

At level 6, the challenge is to work through your innermost issues and find acceptance and resolution so that you can let go of this need to explain and understand your tinnitus. I admit this sounds like a tall order, but if you are at this level your goals in life are much more likely to be about finding peace and satisfaction.

At lower levels it helps to know how tinnitus works and what we do to perpetuate it. It can be really comforting to understand what is happening to you and how to let go of tinnitus. Here, however, in order to move into a deeper sense of peace, it helps to let go of the need to check up on tinnitus. I feel it is much more useful to work with the felt sense of the body. Once we learn to focus on responses that are real and alive inside us, we can work with something that is 100 per cent authentic and a part of us and get direct responses inside. If you stay with how you feel, and work through your internal responses, you will be working as closely to maximum health as possible. Your body is the best doctor you have. Give it the right attention and it will show you what needs to happen.

It's simple, your body is constantly showing you how it is reacting, providing you with one of the clearest and reliably honest streams of information you've got. Use this information to guide you.

Developing your energetic awareness with meditation and having deep body-work therapies like craniosacral therapy or core process work will help you get in touch with this inner intelligence. It is amazing and humbling. I really hope you get a chance to connect with it.

Technique 8: Breathing technique

This is a breathing exercise I have adapted slightly from a lecture given by Dr Leon Chaitow, a professor of health at Westminster University, London. He has dedicated many years of study to health in general and has done a lot of research on of breathing. It is amazing that in just a couple of minutes you can feel an instant calming and centring effect. If you are in a panic, or need to focus away from something, or just want to settle in any situation, please try this.

Start by breathing out through a small hole in your lips, as if blowing through a straw. Feel the pressure in your abdomen as you make a slight effort. This is your diaphragm that has to work for you to do this. Keep on blowing out until you know you want to breath back in, then stop for a second.

Close your lips, and then let go and relax. Have a holiday! As you do this, still with your lips shut, feel the air rush in back through your nose and fill your abdomen. Feel your belly really filling up. Then go back to the beginning again and start blowing out through your lips again.

The first few times you do this you may get a bit dizzy. If this happens, just go back to breathing normally for a few breaths and then try again. I recommend taking just ten of these breaths at a time but practising this often. Slowly as you keep revisiting this technique your breath starts to become more and more centred in the belly. This is where we breathe when we are relaxed and calm.

You can always tell a stressed out person because they breathe in their upper chest and you can often see the shoulders going up and down.

The best thing about this technique that the most important stuff happens when your lips are closed and you are not doing anything – ie when the air *is rushing in all by itself. Feel how the air wants to rush freely down and fill your lower belly.*

This technique is brilliant for letting go of those annoying thought patterns that can take over some times. Changing the focus from thinking to how you are breathing can massively shift your ability to concentrate clearly. This technique helps you practice how to let go with each and every breath. It also changes the oxygen/carbon dioxide balance in every cell of your body. Over a period of time the rate of gas exchange becomes less extreme, and levels out. Instead of taking in masses of oxygen and expelling masses of carbon dioxide, you start exchanging less and less urgently so that the who body can settle and relax more. Try this and notice how you are breathing. I use it every time I need to gather my thoughts or want to calm down.

Level 7: **Liberated**

When I think back over the journey I have been on with tinnitus I am amazed how much my life has changed for the better. For me this condition has behaved like a spiritual guide because it is directly responsible for helping me find a genuine sense of health, well-being, and strength. I can honestly say I am happier now than I have ever been, and if you had told me this would happen when I was down at level one, I would have laughed at you incredulously and growled, "No way!"

As the resting daily focus has moved down from the head into my body, I have started feeling things that I would never have dreamt possible just a few years ago. Before I used to spend the whole time in my thoughts and with all my attention in and around my head. These days I feel centred around my heart a lot of the time and when I walk down the street, or sit with people nearby, I can feel a strong interaction happening between us, often with a focus in my heart area. It feels like a magnetic connection or a gentle push pull. It seems independent from my thought process and gives me valuable information that can be very different to what I think. In fact I rely on my felt sense much more than my thoughts these days if I need to make a decision. The felt sense is much more reliable than my neurotic mind!

All this work has opened up an awareness of the space beyond my physical body – the transpersonal space. Sitting with people I can feel resonance in the space between us, and that is inspiring. Tinnitus has led me into a way of being that is very different to living in a tight, thought-packed head. It is very comforting to get a sense of what the larger picture is like and the connectedness of everything. It fills you with awe and gratitude and lets you experience a deep sense that everything is alright.

I wish I could show you what this is like. Well, as a therapist I guess I can start to. In the meantime I encourage you to continue on your journey of finding peace inside your body. Tinnitus is such an obvious guide to help you along the way towards this goal. As soon as you listen to it in a positive way, you can move towards what is right for you. With support and encouragement the relationship with tinnitus will change from a horrible tyrant that seems to be in control, to a useful guide that is leading you into better health and awareness.

If you let tinnitus help you, slowly you will feel clearer and more aware inside. Deep, careful work like Core Process Psychotherapy or Craniosacral Therapy, or learning how to meditate and focus inside allows you to open up to a larger experience of an interconnected sense of self. Please know that with therapeutic support it is possible to drop into very deep states of calm. As you get in touch with what is going on behind the scenes you can really start to know stillness.

You can become aware of a vibrant state of peace and calm where you feel your centre really clearly, your mind is calm and focussed and you feel very connected to things around you. It is deeply inspiring to touch into these states of being because it can help us shift into a new level of awareness.

Ken Wilber's books: "A Theory of Everything," "No boundary," and "One Taste" provide a very clear understanding of how our level of awareness can change dramatically as we progress through our lives. It is amazing what happens to our sense of self when we really do settle into a deeper stillness. "The Heart of the Buddha's Teaching," by Thich Nhat Hanh, gives us a clear insight into the notion of self and how Buddhism provides a path out of suffering back to well-being. Indeed any spiritual foundation provides invaluable support that helps us let go on a deep level. I personally would encourage anyone to find this kind of support.

I often think of tinnitus as a symptom which, if it could talk, it would say, "Listen to your body, listen to yourself, listen to what is going on inside. Pay attention to this." That is what tinnitus is trying to do, isn't it? It gets people listening to themselves like nothing else does. It gets you to focus inside. Once you do this properly, tinnitus changes.

Personally I don't think this is any coincidence. As a craniosacral therapist myself, I have learnt to have a deep respect for symptoms. They are often a direct link back to health, because they are showing where the problem is. All we need to do is really pay attention to them and notice what they are trying to communicate to us. This is not such a far-fetched idea, if you think about it. If there is pain, then there's something wrong. Owch!

Not good. We need to focus on it. That is what the body is trying to achieve – get our attention in that one place. It does this effortlessly. Unfortunately we often do the opposite and try and blank out the pain with painkillers. Managing pain is one thing, but turning a blind eye to it and pretending that everything is OK is not healthy and is asking for more complicated trouble at a later stage.

The more we focus on how our body feels, the more we understand how well we are or what needs seeing to. Read Eugene Gendlin's book "Focusing," for a very readable and approachable way into this territory. I am grateful to my own tinnitus for showing me this challenging but rewarding path back to health. It really has made me change my diet, exercise, sleeping, social, and resting patterns enormously. It has been an incredibly accurate guide showing exactly what is right for me.

It is no exaggeration to say that tinnitus has been the best doctor, teacher, therapist, friend and guide that I have ever had. What makes it so good is that it is spot on for me, tailor-made for my own needs and nobody else's.

Because tinnitus arises in your body, and is really just an auditory feed-back connecting you directly with the state of your nervous system, you are learning to work directly with what is best for your body. What could be better than that?

So while we are waiting for the magic pill to intervene and switch off this highly intelligent and useful mechanism, leaving us in silence (great), but also in the dark about what causes it in the first place (not so great), in the meantime I encourage you to start working on how you feel inside, and feel better! Its all here, right now inside your body.

My aim in writing this book is to show you a way which works. It makes sense. Many people go through this process of getting better all the time. The only thing that stops you going in the same direction is you! Keep an eye on the saboteur here. Become very suspicious of your own behaviour when you start thinking, "oh this worked for him, but it won't for me, I can't be bothered, I'm too tired, oh its too expensive, I'm waiting for the tinnitus pill to be invented, my doctor said nothing helps, maybe next week." Look through these thoughts and ask yourself what you really want underneath. Maybe you have more choice than you think.

I sincerely wish researchers well. It will be very useful to know exactly which parts of the brain are involved. The work being done on the limbic system is very exciting. The more we know about the engine that we are all driving – ie our bodies, the better. Tinnitus usually arises because of the way the driver is driving the engine, rather than a problem with the engine itself. Drive too fast or put too much strain on it and the engine will flounder and make unhealthy noises. It is not sensible to put more sound-proofing over the engine to smother these noises out. This is not dealing with the problem. Surely it's better to help the driver slow down and drive in a way that keeps the engine functional for the longest time with as few problems as possible. The good news is that there is one important difference between a car engine and a body: if we give our bodies space and our full attention, they repair themselves. Bodies are designed to work as well as possible and to do the best they can to function at maximum health. Healing happens when we rest, eat well, feel happy and well in ourselves and when we switch off and let go. Cars need mechanics.

At this level, you know yourself and your body well and you are aware how you drive it. The challenge here is to open to the larger picture and help others overcome their own suffering. As your tinnitus gets better and better you can share this approach with others. We need to be strong in the face of all the negativity, and lack of understanding surrounding tinnitus. When we hear people say, "There is nothing you can do about it," we need to reply from our own experience, "Well actually there is masses you can do about tinnitus. I have got better and I know how this happened."

I can only hope that health practitioners stop saying tinnitus cannot be cured. This is very harmful and does not help anyone. Please learn how to help tinnitus first before delivering devastating messages to disempowered people who cannot cope with them. This increases suffering. Send people with tinnitus to practitioners who can provide them with proper care and support, and who can bring their nervous system out of overwhelm and back towards ideal resting states. Keep it simple. Send people with tinnitus to practitioners who will help them discover well-being. This is already a huge step in the right direction.

The magic miracle cure for tinnitus is to help bring people out of red-alert mode back towards a neutral resting place. This involves bringing the parasympathetic nervous system back into balance with the sympathetic nervous symptom. This is simple physiology, and is something that alternative practitioners and body-based psychotherapists do everyday.

Technique 9: Orienting to midline

This is a technique that is widely known amongst the Craniosacral Therapy, Core Process Psychotherapy community and people who meditate. Particular thanks to Maura and Franklyn Sills of the Karuna Institute in Devon, UK, who helped clarify this for me from their own deep centre of awareness. (I thoroughly recommend their courses for anyone who is interested in finding out what're really going on inside.)

The intention is to develop an awareness of your midline, your central vertical axis. This is the part of you that connects your crown down your spine to your tailbone. Awareness of your midline can help you feel really centred and clear, and provide a sense of connection to other people in a manageable way, especially when you come into contact with challenging situations.

All you need to do is sit vertically and comfortably with a straight but not rigid back. Feel your sitting bones on the chair or cushion. Feel your head and notice if it is directly above your tailbone. Sit comfortably with this sense of head to tailbone and feel your way up and down the spine. Become aware of how vertical you are and what the spine feels like.

Does it feel straight? Can you feel one half of your body closer in to the middle than the other? Maybe you have a sense that your midline is slightly ahead of you, or that it is very hard to feel at all. Just notice how it is for you. Become aware of whether it is clear, out of focus, narrow, broad, floaty, strong, vague, and so on.

▶

Once you have a felt sense of this midline, extend it down into the ground like a plumb-line. Imagine a strong connection down through the floor into the earth. Try and get a felt sense of this like a fluid and magnetic density coming out of you and linking into the ground. Notice if anything starts feeling different in the base of your spine as you do this.

Sometimes you can feel floaty feelings up and down your spine. It becomes much stronger and easier to feel if you are surrounded by other people doing the same thing. Your local meditation centre would be a good place to explore this. If you are in the presence of someone else that has a very clear midline, then you may naturally come into resonance with them and find it becomes easier to feel in yourself.

When you have a clear midline you feel grounded and connected to the earth and have a strong sense of being centred. From this space it is easier to notice what is going on inside you and around you. If you lean forward, you can feel the line moving through the earth backwards. If you lean to the left, you can feel a pendulum of energetic connection swinging to the right beneath you. If you lean backwards, it moves forwards under you. The midline is just a continuation of your own central axis and moves in line with that.

Try extending your awareness above your head a little and see if there is a sense of midline continuing up.

Get a sense of where your focus is along the midline. By this I mean is there any particularly clear part of this central axis that feels more intensely aware than elsewhere. Is it behind your eyes, behind your heart, at the base of your abdomen, or maybe above your head? Notice how this focus is. Does it stay in one place or is it shifting?

When you get a sense of your midline, you can move from here out into the day from a centred and manageable place, and feel this centre interacting

> *with people and experiences around you. Its like you respond to things from the whole of you, rather than from just your thinking self, or a part of your body.*

So we have come to the end of our journey. I hope that I have inspired you to start taking a look inside yourself and find out how you really feel inside. My advice is always please seek the support of a therapeutic relationship. There is nothing that helps more than being supported by someone else. Just like a little baby needs a loving mother to grow and develop into a happy and balanced person, as adults we still have needs for support and care that only come from being in relationship with another person.

Stick the matrix somewhere where you can see it and get to know it, eg on the fridge or a cupboard. This will help you recognise how you are making progress, and can help motivate you to keep on going. Use the techniques regularly and find out what most helps you.

All your patterns are sitting in your body right now. Get in touch with how you feel just as you are right now and they will probably start changing right before your eyes. I still find this extraordinary.

My advice to you is to get in touch with your body as often as you can. Explore these techniques. Discover your inner felt-sense and learn to work with it. This will bring you closer to your normal state of maximum health.

As you let go more and more into the realm of no resistance, tinnitus ceases to be possible and vanishes! I wish you the best of health and, above all, peace.

For details on where to find a practitioner of craniosacral therapy or core process psychotherapy, please go to the website:

www.craniosacral.co.uk

http://www.karuna-institute.co.uk/referrals.html

To find a practitioner in any therapy I recommend contacting the relevant association first. Most organisations have a website for this and can been found using a search engine on the net. Each association website often provides lists of registered practitioners. Taking this route usually provides a certain guarantee of quality and standards.

Feed-back is welcome. Please send it to:

Julian Cowan Hill
Apartment 15
27 Sheldon Square
London
W2 6DW

Or email: info@juliancowanhill.co.uk

My website is juliancowanhill.co.uk

Bibliography

Nancy Appleton, *Lick the Sugar Habit*, 1996, Avery Books

Rollin Becker, *Life in Motion: the Osteopathic Vision of Rollin Becker*, 1997, Stillness Press

Chaitow, Breadley & Gilbert, *Multidisciplinary Approaches to Breathing Pattern Disorders*, 2002, Harcourt

Eugene Gendlin, *Focusing: How to Open Up Your Deeper Feelings and Intuition*, 2003, Ebury Press

Eugene Gendlin, *Focussing-Oriented Psychotherapy*, 1996, Guildford Press

Thich Nhat Hanh, *The Heart of the Buddha's Teaching: Transforming Suffering into Peace, Joy and*. 1998 Rider Books

Karen Kissel Wegela, *How to be a Help Instead of a Nuisance: Practical Approaches to Giving Support, Service and Encouragement to Others*, 1996, Shambala

Jack Kornfield, *A Path with Heart*, 1993, Random House

Peter Levine, *Wating the Tiger: Healing Trauma*, 1997, North Atlantic Books

Arnold Mindell, *Working on Yourself Alone: Inner Dreambody Work*, 1990, Arkana

Caroline Myss, *Sacred Contracts: Awakening Your Divine Potential*, 2004, Hay House

Rosemary Payne, *Relaxation Techniques: A Practical Handbook for the Health Care Professional*, 1995, Harcourt

Babette Rothschild, *The Body Remembers: The Psychophysiology of Trauma and Trauma Treatment*, 2000 Norton Professional Books

Ken Wilber, *A Theory of Everything: An Integral Vision for Business*, Politics, Science and Spirituality, 2001, Shambala

Ken Wilber, *No Boundary: Eastern and Western Approaches to Personal Growth*, 1979, Shambala

Zweig and Abrams, *Meeting the Shadow: the Hidden Power of the Dark Side of Human Nature*, 1990 Tarcher Putnam

Printed in Poland
by Amazon Fulfillment
Poland Sp. z o.o., Wrocław